The Princess Who Believed in Fairy Tales

Marcia Grad

A Marcia Grad Publication

Melvin Powers
Wilshire Book Company

12015 Sherman Road, No. Hollywood, CA 91605

ISBN 0-87980-436-X
Library of Congress Catalog Card Number 94-061729
Printed in the United States of America

Contents

PART I

Chapter One

Someday My Prince Will Come

ONCE upon a time there was a delicate, little golden-haired princess named Victoria, who believed with all her heart that fairy tales come true and princesses live happily ever after. She believed in the magic of wishes, the triumph of good over evil, and the power of love to conquer all—a philosophy well founded in fairy-tale wisdom.

Ever since the little princess could remember, she had snuggled—all rosy and warm from her evening bubble bath—under her fluffy pink quilts and into mounds of downy pillows and listened to the queen read her bedtime stories about beautiful damsels in distress. Whether dressed in tatters, cursed to a hundred-year sleep, trapped in a tower, or the victim of some other dismal situation, the fair maiden was always daringly rescued by a courageous, handsome, charming prince. The little princess savored every word her mother read and night after night, drifted off to sleep spinning wonderful fairy tales of her own.

"Will my prince ever come?" she asked the queen one night, her gentle amber eyes wide with wonder and innocence.

"Yes, dear," the queen replied. "Someday."

"And will he be big and strong and brave and handsome and charming?" the little princess asked.

"Of course. All that you dream of and more. He will

be the light of your life, your reason for being. So it is destined."

"And will we live happily ever after, forever and ever, like in the fairy tales?" she asked dreamily, tilting her head and clasping her hands to her cheek.

The queen drew her fingers slowly through the little princess's hair with long, tender strokes. "Just like in the fairy tales," she replied. "Now it is time to sleep." She kissed the little princess lightly on the forehead, then withdrew from the room, quietly pulling the door closed behind her.

"You can come out now. It's safe," the little princess whispered, leaning over the side of her bed and lifting the bed ruffle so Timothy Vandenberg III could come out of hiding. "Come on, boy," she said.

Her furry friend jumped up and took his usual spot beside her. He didn't look at all like a Timothy Vandenberg III. He looked more like a Rags. But the little princess loved him as if he had been the most royal of dogs. She gave him a big hug. Contented, they both went to sleep.

Each day the little princess dabbed on some of the queen's herbal-berry cheek color and dressed up in one of her mother's ball gowns and high-heeled dancing shoes, which the little princess pretended were glass slippers. Holding the massive skirts off the floor, she clopped around her bedroom practicing batting her eyelashes coyly, sighing demurely, and saying, "I always knew you'd come, my prince," and "Why certainly. I would be honored to be your bride." Then she acted out the rescue scenes from her favorite fairy tales, reciting the lines from memory.

The little princess practiced diligently in preparation of her prince's arrival, never tiring of playing her role. By the time her seventh birthday came, she was quite accomplished at batting her eyes, sighing, and accepting proposals of marriage.

At supper, after the little princess made her secret birthday wish and blew out the candles on her chocolate fudge cake, the queen rose and approached her, an elaborately wrapped package in her hands.

"Your father and I think that you are now old enough to appreciate this special gift. It has been handed down from mother to daughter for generations. I was exactly your age when my mother gave it to me for my birthday. And we hope one day to see you give it to a daughter of your own."

The queen placed the package in her daughter's outstretched hands. The little princess was filled with anticipation, but in her usual fashion, she slowly slipped off the ribbon and bow so she could add them undamaged to her collection. Then she loosened the wrapping paper so as not to tear it and slowly pulled out an antique music box with two little figurines on top, an elegant couple posed in the waltz position.

"Oh, look!" she exclaimed, lightly touching the figurines with her fingertips. "It's a fair maiden and her prince!"

"Turn it on, Princess," the king said.

Careful not to wind too far, she turned the little key. Tinkling sounds of "Someday My Prince Will Come" floated into the air, and the elegant couple began to revolve around and around.

"My favorite song!" the little princess cried.

The queen was pleased. "It is a promise of your future. A reminder of what will be."

"I love it," the little princess answered, mesmerized by the music and dancing figurines. "Thank you! Thank you!"

Victoria couldn't wait to get upstairs to her bedroom that night to play in private with the music box and to plan and dream with Vicky—her invisible very best friend ever, who the king and queen insisted was imaginary.

"Hurry up, Victoria," Vicky said excitedly as soon as the bedroom door was shut. "Turn it on!"

"I *am* hurrying," Victoria replied, setting the music box down on her dressing table and turning the key.

Vicky began to hum as the music of "Someday My Prince Will Come" filled the room. "Come on, Victoria, I feel like dancing."

"I don't know if we should. I think—"

"You think too much. Come on."

The little princess walked over to the full-length, brass-framed mirror that stood in the corner of her pink and white bedroom. Whenever she looked into that mirror, the reflection that looked back at her always made her feel so beautiful that she was moved to dance. Now, with the music playing, she could not resist. Gracefully she turned this way and that, swooping down low and reaching up high in a spirited dance that came from somewhere deep inside her. Timothy Vandenberg III danced, too, in a fashion, playfully turning round and round, and every so often, over and over.

The upstairs maid came in to turn down the bed, as was her duty. So thoroughly was she enjoying the little princess's joyful dance that she took much longer than was her habit.

Suddenly the queen appeared at the doorway. The maid was flustered at having been discovered watching the little princess rather than attending to her duties.

Timothy, immediately sensing the queen's presence, dashed under the bed to safety.

But so absorbed in her dance was the little princess that she didn't notice the queen until she heard her ordering the maid to leave. She froze right in the middle of one of her best twirls.

"Honestly, Victoria!" the queen said. "How could you put on that undignified display?"

The little princess was mortified. How could anything that felt so good be so bad? she wondered.

"If you want to dance," the queen said, "you must learn to do it properly. The Regal Studio of Performing Arts has superb instructors of ballet, a pursuit far more befitting a princess than bobbing up and down, flailing one's arms around like a lowly commoner—in front of a commoner, no less!"

At that moment the little princess silently vowed that she would never again, as long as she lived, do her "Someday My Prince Will Come" dance in front of anyone—with one exception, and that was Timothy. But he was different. Since finding him wandering around the palace grounds hungry and abandoned, she had trusted him with many private things, and he always loved her anyway—unlike some people she knew.

The queen calmed herself and stayed for her daughter's nightly bubble bath. She helped the little princess into her puffed-sleeve lilac nightgown, then sat down beside her on the big, white-lace canopy bed. She picked up the book of fairy tales from the top of the night table and began to read aloud.

Soon the little princess was caught up once again in the magical world of happily ever after. Her stomach settled down, and the upsetting incident completely faded from her mind.

Chapter Two

The Little Princess and the Royal Code

THE little princess strolled down the narrow, winding path of the palace rose garden, struggling to carry a box that held three small pots of blooming red rosebushes, a trowel, some fertilizer, gardening gloves, a sprinkling can, and a large bathing towel from the palace linen supply. All around her, bright pink, white, yellow, and red rosebuds were gently opening their newborn petals toward the sun, their perfume rising to the treetops. Her happy heart sang, and soon so did she as she spread out the towel next to a patch of earth ripe for planting and knelt upon it. The palace head gardener had taught her well. She knew what to do, and she did it without getting so much as a spot of dirt on her ruffly white pinafore.

By the time she slipped the first plant into the earth, the sweetness of her song had brought birds from the trees to gather around and sing in harmony with her.

After she finished her planting and had returned to the palace, her melody filled the royal foyer—as did the birds that had followed her.

There was so much singing and chirping that the little princess didn't hear the king come through a door near the end of the long hallway.

"Victoria," he said angrily as he marched toward her. "Stop this ruckus right now! Haven't I talked to you repeatedly about this? You just don't listen!"

The little princess was startled by the king's sudden presence. "I'm sorry, Father," she said nervously over the cheeping, tweeting birds. "I'm sorry if my singing is—"

"For the birds," he said. "That's what it is. A fact attested to by those infernal creatures congregating on the grounds and flying in and out of the palace windows, making a commotion every time you start up those vocal antics." He waved his arms, shooing away the birds. "Get them out of here at once! I have a roomful of foreign dignitaries, and we can hardly talk over this racket you call singing!"

"Yes, Father," the little princess answered, trying desperately not to sound as if she had been dealt a mortal blow, for she knew well the consequences of getting upset in front of anyone—especially her father.

Satisfied, the king turned and strode toward the door whence he had come, but Timothy Vandenberg III suddenly appeared, barking wildly and darting across his path, and nearly knocked him down. "Guard!" the king yelled. "Remove this mutt from the premises and ensure that he will never return!"

"No, no, Father! Not Timothy! Don't take him away, please!"

"He's nothing but a nuisance, Victoria." He turned to the guard and pointed toward the door. "The mutt goes."

The guard scrambled after Timothy Vandenberg III, who raced first in one direction, then another. As the guard lunged at him, Timothy ran smack into an alabaster pedestal, sending an arrangement of long-stemmed red roses crashing to the marble floor.

The little princess clutched the guard's leg as he snatched the stunned dog. "Please don't take him," she wailed. "Please!"

The queen, who had heard the commotion and hurried

to the foyer to see the cause, grabbed the princess by her arms and pulled her away from the guard. "Victoria, you are to stop your disgraceful behavior this instant! Your father is right. A mutt is an unfit pet for a princess, anyway." She looked around, annoyed. "Look at this mess!"

The little princess held back her own anger and said nothing. But the expression on her face gave her away.

"You know better than that!" the queen said, scrutinizing the little princess's grim face. "Go straight to your room and review the Royal Code, especially the portions referring to ladylike demeanor and improper display of emotions. And do not come out until you have a smile on your face."

The little princess fought the anger that tempted her to bolt from the room. A river of tears swelled in its place as she turned to leave. She choked back all but a few errant droplets, which managed to trickle down her cheeks as she slowly climbed the grand circular staircase that led upstairs to her bedroom.

Once in her room, more tears fell. She looked up at the Royal Code of Feelings and Behavior for Princesses, mounted prominently on the wall over her dressing table. It had been perfectly lettered on white parchment by the palace calligrapher and suitably framed and hung by the palace decorator, per the queen's instructions. It decreed not only how the little princess was expected to look, act, and speak at all times, but also how she was expected to think and feel. And it clearly stated what was unacceptable for her to feel and think, which was often exactly what she *was* feeling and thinking. Nowhere did it explain how to stop. Why did she have to be a princess, anyway? she wondered.

"You think it's my fault like always, don't you, Victoria?" asked Vicky, the little voice that came from somewhere deep within the princess.

"Yes! I've told you a million times we'd get in trouble

if you kept singing and dancing and moping and pouting. You just don't listen!"

"I hate it when you sound like the king," Vicky replied.

"I'm sorry, but I don't know what to do anymore."

"I can follow the Royal Code. Honest. I'll prove it." Vicky raised her right hand, cleared her throat, and solemnly recited, "I promise for sure to follow the Royal Code 'xactly at all times, to be good—no, better than good, perfect, even. Cross my heart and hope to die, kiss a lizard in one try."

"It's not going to work," predicted Victoria.

"Uh-huh. I promised, didn't I?"

"You've promised lots of times."

"But I never said 'cross my heart' before."

"If only the king and queen could understand it's you and not me making all the trouble," Victoria said with a sigh.

"I can't help it if they think I'm 'maginary," Vicky said meekly. "Anyway, it's not gonna happen again. You'll see."

The little princess didn't feel much like eating supper that evening. She would gladly have not appeared but knew better. And she knew better than to show up with a long face. So although smiling on the outside while crying on the inside was one of the most difficult lessons of all, Victoria was determined to learn it.

She forced herself to practice smiling into her full-length, brass-framed mirror. The king had often told her that her smile was a gift to behold—but it certainly didn't look like it then. Frustrated with the effort, she finally settled for plastering a halfhearted grin on her face and headed down to the royal dining room.

At the supper table, the little princess toyed with her food. She was unusually quiet.

"Is something wrong with your supper?" the king asked.

The little princess shifted uncomfortably in her seat.

"Princess, did you hear me?"

"Yes," she replied softly.

"Yes, *what?*"

"Yes, I heard you," she answered respectfully.

"Well then?"

"There's nothing wrong with my supper, Father," she replied, listlessly dragging her fork back and forth through a mound of noodles.

"Apparently there is a problem," the queen said. "What is it, pray tell?"

The little princess looked up from her plate. "Nothing," she answered, putting down her fork and twisting the fine linen napkin on her lap.

"Victoria, I want an explanation now," the king demanded. "And this had better not have anything to do with that mangy mutt."

She began to fidget and cleared her throat several times. "I'm afraid to tell you," she mumbled at last.

The king and queen continued to press her. Finally, unable to tolerate their glaring eyes any longer, she admitted what was tearing at her heart. "I want Timothy back."

"Your father made it very clear—"

"Please!" the king snapped at his wife. "I'll handle this." Agitated, he rose from the table and paced back and forth, his hands clasped behind his back.

"Please, Father," the little princess blurted out. "It wasn't Timothy's fault he almost knocked you down. He always gets crazy when Vicky is upset. And when you yelled at her about her singing—"

"Vicky again! Your mother and I have told you that you can't blame some imaginary playmate for your being the way you are!"

"I'm not," Victoria answered timidly. "Vicky isn't imaginary. She's real."

"You are too old for this," the queen said. "It is high time you learned the difference between what is real and what is not. People will begin to talk!"

Victoria frowned. "I don't care what people say. Vicky is real. She talks and laughs and cries and feels things. She loves to sing and dance and dream and—"

The king was furious. "So *she's* the one who attracts scores of messy birds with her vocal antics and makes a spectacle of herself in front of the servants! And *she's* the one who's responsible for the mutt being underfoot and who cries and carries on when things don't suit her! Is that what you're telling me, Victoria?"

"But—but—you don't understand," Victoria said in her tiniest voice. "You're always mad at her, but she's really wonderful. She's cute and sweet and fun and nice and—and she's the very best friend I've ever had. Can't you try to—"

The king reacted as he always did in such situations. He sternly reprimanded her, shaking his finger vigorously in front of her nose. His face turned bright red, and he broke out in a rash as his voice thundered in her ears. "You're much too delicate, Victoria! Too sensitive. Too afraid of your own shadow. Such a dreamer. What's the matter with you? Why can't you be like other royal children!" Then he threw up his hands in frustration. "What have I done to deserve this?"

The queen tried to calm him, which, as usual, only made matters worse. The two of them argued about the little princess as if she weren't even there. Wishing she could just disappear, she lowered her head, stared at the tablecloth in front of her, and avoided their eyes. She couldn't bear to see her reflection in them—a reflection that time and time again showed her what was wrong with her.

Soon their icy stares and angry voices pummeled her again. "Look at us when we talk to you, Victoria!" demanded the king.

She looked up with big, frightened eyes, barely able to hear their words over the loud noises Vicky was making to shut out their voices.

After an agonizing few minutes, the queen said, "See what you have done now, Victoria! Your father is all upset again. Princesses are supposed to be strong—models of royal perfection. Surely you know that by now. There is a right and a wrong way to be, a right and a wrong way to do, and a right and a wrong way to feel. And you are going to learn the difference, young lady, once and for all! Now go to your room and stay there. And for heaven's sake, get that look off your face!"

Victoria was shaken by the whole ordeal, and Vicky's yelling was giving her a terrible headache. As a matter of fact, Vicky had *become* a terrible headache.

Vicky continued to babble on as the little princess climbed the winding palace staircase. "If princesses are all they say, we prob'ly aren't a real princess at all. I bet the stork brought them the wrong baby. That's it! I know it. Victoria . . . Victoria," Vicky repeated, her voice getting louder. "Aren't you talking to me?"

"You!" Victoria screamed accusingly the moment they got into the bedroom. "*You* are the one who's sensitive and afraid of things. You're the one who's always feeling things you aren't supposed to and dreaming of things that probably won't ever happen. You even make me blab things we aren't supposed to! *You're* the one not minding the Royal Code, and *I'm* the one getting in all the trouble!"

"I am what I am," Vicky mumbled so quietly that Victoria had to strain to hear her. "And what I am isn't good enough. You'll never get along with them as long as I'm around. I should run away and never come back."

"What am I going to do?" Victoria moaned. "You have to be kept away from the king and queen. Maybe if you stay hidden underneath the bed from now on—"

"Like Timothy? A dog? I don't wanna stay under there. Anyway, it's *his* hiding place, and I want *him* to stay there, like always."

"I can't do anything about getting him back, but I *can* do something about *you*," Victoria replied. "I have to hide you somewhere, and under the bed is the only place I can think of."

Vicky agreed, although she was far from happy about it. But once safely hidden under the bed, she talked on and on about how the Royal Code wasn't fair. How the king and queen were mean and hated her. How lonely she was going to be under the bed all day. How she wasn't good enough to be anyone's best friend. And how she still felt like running away and never coming back.

Later that evening, too upset for her nightly bubble bath and fairy tale, Victoria turned away both the maid and the queen when they came to her bedroom door, and she settled into bed for the night with Vicky still talking.

Unable to sleep, she finally insisted that Vicky be quiet. Instead, the distraught little girl crawled out of hiding and climbed into bed with Victoria. She buried her face deep into the pile of pillows and cried and cried. Her tears soaked the silky bedcovers until they dripped onto the floor.

"Stop it!" Victoria insisted in a hushed voice. "I can't stand this anymore. You're getting everything all wet. Besides, someone'll hear you. What's the matter with you, anyway? You know very well there's a right and a wrong way to be, a right and a wrong way to do, and a right and a wrong way to feel. And you're going to learn the difference, young lady, once and for all!"

"What're you gonna do?" Vicky asked with a sniffle.

"What I should've done a long time ago. I'm going to

put you where you can't pop up and cause trouble for me anymore!"

"I thought you were my friend, but you're not!" Vicky yelled back at her. "You're mean, just like the king and queen."

"Don't blame *me*. This is all *your* fault! I told you to stay away from them," Victoria said, tumbling out of bed and nearly slipping as her bare feet hit a puddle of tears. She turned on the bedside lamp. "Get in there right now!" she ordered, pointing at one of the extra wardrobe closets on the other side of the room. "And I don't want to hear any crying or complaining, either."

With that, she pulled Vicky from the bed, dragged her screaming across the room, shoved her into the closet, and slammed the door. Then in the same tone of voice she had heard the queen use many times, she said, "I'm doing this for your own good, Vicky." She placed the gold key in the lock and turned it determinedly.

"Don't lock it! I won't come out. I promise, Victoria. Cross my—"

"Your promises don't mean anything."

Victoria tossed the key into her white wooden hope chest with hand-carved clusters of roses at the corners. "I know you. You'll start babbling and whining and opening the closet door to say this or that whenever you feel like it and—"

"You can't just hide me away," Vicky yelled through the door. "We belong together. We promised to be best friends no matter what, 'member?"

"That was before you became my worst enemy," Victoria said.

"Victoria, please, please let me out of here," Vicky called, desperately pounding on the door. "I need you. We're s'posed to be together always. Don't leave me all alone! I'm afraid, Victoria. I'll be good. I'll do anything you say. Please, let me out!"

Victoria climbed back into her big canopy bed. Alone, drained and as limp as the noodles at supper, she pressed her puffy pillows tightly to her ears to muffle the sound of Vicky's sobs coming through the closet door. Eventually the sobs turned to whimpers. And finally the whimpers turned to silence. Victoria pulled up a corner of her fluffy quilt and rubbed its softness against her cheek, wearily slipping into a private little world where all bad things simply drift away.

♥ ♥

The next morning before the little princess had arisen, the king appeared at her bedroom door with a red rose, a sheepish smile, and a bulging bagful of Thinkertoys—a colorful wooden building set painstakingly whittled by the royal toy maker.

"Good morning, Princess," he said, waltzing into her room and sitting next to her on the bed. "I see we're going to get a late start on building the playhouse today."

"The playhouse?— Oh, it's Sunday," she said, so exhausted that she could hardly sit up. "I don't feel like it today, Father."

"Come on, Princess. We never miss a Sunday, do we? Here," he said, holding the rose out in front of her. "I thought this might bring that lovely smile back to those little rosebud lips."

She looked at the rose and at the king, who was giving her a pleading grin. As many times as this had happened, she still had trouble knowing what to think or do or feel.

The king reached over and pulled her up onto his lap. He wrapped his arms around her, enveloping her in the massive sleeves of his soft velvet robe. "Oh, my darling daughter. You truly are a beauty," he said. And she could feel his chest puff up with pride as he hugged her tightly.

"I love you, Father," the little princess said.

The king looked down at the golden-haired prize in his arms. "I love you, too, Princess," he answered. And she knew he meant it.

As was their weekly ritual, the little princess and the king used the toy maker's building set to construct a playhouse. When they had finished, the princess crawled inside and sat cross-legged, while the king lay on his stomach on the floor, his head and shoulders barely fitting through the opening they called the front door. There they drank hot chocolate together brought to them in large matching mugs by the palace day cook.

Tipping the mug to his mouth while leaning on his elbows was no easy task for the king. From time to time, drops of the hot liquid trickled down his arms and into the sleeves of his royal robe, but he never mentioned it.

Everything was going so well that Victoria decided to try making peace, once and for all, about Vicky. But it was a disaster. As soon as she mentioned Vicky's name, the king was so angry that he jumped up, knocking down the playhouse in the process.

"There *is* no Vicky, do you hear me!" he roared. "I give up! You're impossible!"

The little princess covered her head with her arms as the small, colored wooden building pieces showered down around her.

"I'm sorry, Father," she managed to say in a quivering voice.

But the king stormed out, leaving the princess stunned, sitting on the floor in a pile of rubble.

Chapter Three

Beyond the Palace Gardens

EVERYTHING seemed so different with Vicky gone, Victoria thought, as she gazed out her bedroom window late one afternoon. Her eyes found their way to a wispy tree standing alone atop a little hill just beyond the palace gardens. She had never paid much attention to it before, but that day it seemed to her that the tree looked sad and lonely out there all by itself. A solitary tear escaped from the corner of one eye and trickled down Victoria's cheek. It's so sad to be lonely, she thought. And it's so lonely to be sad without being able to tell anyone about it. As she thought about how she shouldn't be feeling either one—lonely or sad—her head began to ache.

Things had not been going as well as she had anticipated since locking up Vicky. Following the Royal Code was a lot easier in Vicky's absence, but being perfect was still a monumental task.

For some reason she was unable to take her eyes from the tree. Feeling drawn there, she wandered down the stairs, out of the palace, and through the gardens, oblivious to the beauty that had once filled her with joy. When she reached the top of the little hill beyond, she sat down on the hard ground beneath the lone tree and leaned against its trunk, holding her aching head in her hands.

"I'll never, ever, be good enough—no matter how hard

I try," Victoria said with a sigh.

"Good enough for what?" asked a voice.

She bolted upright and looked all around. "Who said that?"

"Who? Who? I did," the voice answered.

It seemed to be coming from the tree. "Who are you?"

"Who are *you*?" the voice repeated. "*That* is the question."

"Okay. I'll tell you first," Victoria said, rising slowly so as not to make her headache worse. She curtsied her best curtsy. "I am Princess Victoria, daughter of the king and queen of this kingdom. I live in the palace on the other side of the gardens. I am number one in my class at the Royal Elementary Academy of Excellence. I try my hardest to follow the Royal Code of Feelings and Behavior for Princesses at all times. I'm a lot better at planting roses than I am at softball. I used to have a dog named Timothy Vandenberg the Third. And sometimes I get really bad headaches—like now."

"That's all very interesting, Princess, but it isn't who you are."

"It is too! I ought to know who I am," Victoria replied indignantly.

"Everyone *ought* to know who they are, but few do."

"You're getting me all confused."

"Knowing you are confused is the first step to getting unconfused."

"I'm arguing with a tree?" Victoria mumbled to herself. "Maybe Mother and Father are right. Maybe I *can't* tell what's real and what's not."

She looked up at the mass of branches hanging above her. "Please, tell me you talked to me, Mr. Tree," Victoria pleaded. "You did, didn't you?"

"The answer to your question is yes—and no," the voice replied.

"You *do* talk, Mr. Tree! You *do!*"

"Things are not always as they appear, Princess."

At that moment an owl descended, floating to the ground like a wayward feather. He clapped his wings briefly, straightened the stethoscope that dangled from his neck, and carefully placed a black bag at his feet.

"Allow me to introduce myself," he said in a most dignified manner. "I am Henry Herbert Hoot, D.H. My friends call me Doc."

"Oh, no! A talking tree and now a talking owl with a name like Henry Herbert Hoot? I guess I *can't* tell what's real from what's not, after all."

"On the contrary, I'm as real as a fairy tale to a princess— Ah, that reminds me of a song," he said, obviously delighted. "Of course lots of things remind me of songs."

With that, he reached into his black bag, pulled out a straw hat, which he patted on his head, and a miniature banjo. He began strumming and singing:

> So real is a fairy tale to a princess,
> As real as great power to a king—

"Stop, please," Victoria moaned, clasping her hands to her head. "I'm sorry, but it hurts too much to listen to music right now."

"Perhaps you wouldn't hurt so much if you would listen to your own music more often," the owl suggested.

"I don't feel much like singing anymore."

"I was referring to the music of your heart."

"I don't know what that is. What does an owl know about hearts, anyway?"

"Quite a lot, actually," he replied. "As my title, D.H., suggests, I am a doctor of the heart. I specialize in broken ones."

Victoria slumped forward and bowed her head. Finally, in a soft voice, she asked, "How does it feel to have a broken heart?"

"From the sadness in your eyes, I suspect you already know the answer to that," Doc replied, removing his hat and slipping it and the banjo back into the black bag.

"I'm afraid that my heart *is* broken," the little princess choked, her eyes still cast downward.

"Your self-diagnosis is correct."

"Can you fix it? My heart, that is."

"I can't fix it exactly, but I *can* help *you* to do it. Still, it will take more than mere fixing to sweep the sadness from your eyes, Princess."

"But what else is there?"

"Healing."

"Well, then, can you heal my heart?"

"I'm afraid not, Princess. Only *you* can do that."

Victoria frowned. "What kind of a doctor are you if I have to heal my own heart?"

"The same as any other kind. We can fix many things and help to fix others—but the healing we cannot do."

"I don't understand."

"There's a lot you don't understand yet, but you will someday. Now," Doc said, changing the subject, "do you feel better knowing that it was I who talked to you, rather than the tree?"

"Of course not," Victoria replied, her fists resting on her hips. "I can't explain a talking, singing owl who's a doctor any better than I can explain a talking tree."

"Some things need not be explained. They are simply to be experienced."

"Try telling that to my mother if any of the palace guards see me out here talking to no one— Oh, I-I'm sorry," she stammered. "I didn't exactly mean no one. That is—well, you know— Anyway," she said, noticing the sun dipping low on the horizon, "I have to go. When can I come back?"

"Whenever the spirit moves," the owl replied.

"'The spirit moves?' What does that mean?"

"For now, simply know that you may come back anytime you wish."

"You sure say funny things," the little princess said, shaking her head and realizing that it didn't hurt anymore. Then she started down the hill toward the palace, waving and calling good-bye as she went.

As she approached the palace entry, the little princess saw the queen staring out a front bay window. By the time she reached the front door, her mother was holding it open.

"It's almost dark. Where were you, Victoria?"

"I was at the tree," she mumbled.

"Doing what?"

Unfortunately, the Royal Code strictly prohibited lies of any kind. Even little white ones. Even in dire emergencies like this one. Victoria had no choice but to answer truthfully.

"Talking," she replied hesitantly.

"To whom?"

"The tree," she answered, anticipating a scene.

"I suppose that next you will be telling me the tree talked back."

The tone of the queen's voice sent chills cascading down the little princess's spine. "At first. I mean I thought it was the tree, but it was really an owl."

"Honestly, Victoria! This has got to stop. You simply cannot continue telling these outlandish stories. It is high time you got your head out of the clouds."

Victoria wasn't sure what it meant to have one's head in the clouds, but she thought it sounded wonderful.

"I can prove that the owl talks," she said meekly.

"Not another word about any of this, Victoria. And as

for that tree or owl, or whatever—I forbid you to return there. Now this discussion is over." Then the queen turned and briskly walked away.

"Why doesn't she ever believe me?" Victoria asked under her breath. "I *know* that owl talks. I heard it."

But that night she began to wonder if perhaps the queen had been right. After all, who ever heard of a talking owl? A singing doctor, no less, with a banjo and straw hat. Besides, the queen always seemed to be right about everything.

♥ ♥

Each year as she grew older, the princess hoped that the next year would be happier. Of course there were grand balls and elaborate picnics and fun-filled afternoons at polo matches throughout the kingdom, but something always seemed to be missing. Often the princess wistfully watched the birds from her bedroom window as they flitted together from treetop to treetop, singing, belonging, free to be. She imagined what it would feel like to be one of them. To not feel different and alone even when among friends.

As spring followed winter and summer turned to fall, Victoria blossomed into a lovely young woman, graceful and gracious and all that a princess should be.

She graduated with honors from the Royal High Academy of Excellence. But perhaps her greatest achievement was becoming accomplished at saying, doing, thinking, and feeling exactly as the Royal Code dictated.

On the evening of her graduation, the king and queen held a grand celebration in the palace ballroom with lyrical lute players and colorful court jesters. With a sea of distinguished guests looking on, the proud king presented his daughter with a special gift.

"On this momentous occasion," he began, "I proudly

present you with the Royal Family Map—a treasure of immeasurable value that has been responsible for directing the course of our ancestors' royal lives as far back as our lineage has been traced. In the noble tradition of the royal family of this kingdom, you shall follow the path set out herein."

He handed the rolled, graying parchment to the princess. It had a shiny silver band around it and was affixed with the royal seal. Its frayed edges revealed its loyal use by many generations of royal families.

The king lifted his glass of ale and called out, "Long live the royal legacy!"

"Here, here," answered the throng of well-wishers, raising their glasses to the princess. "Long live the royal legacy! Long live the princess! Long live the king and queen!"

When the last of the guests had departed, Victoria returned to her room, kicked off her shoes, and fell onto her bed, thinking about where to put the Royal Family Map for safekeeping. Although she had no doubt as to its authenticity or its usefulness, she didn't expect to ever need it, as she already knew exactly where she was going. First to the Imperial University to get an education befitting a princess and an MRS. degree. Then to a palace of her own with her Prince Charming, to live happily ever after.

She tucked the map away in her hope chest and wandered over to her dressing table, drawn by the sweet aroma of roses the head gardener of the palace had picked fresh for her that morning—as he did every morning. They were perfectly arranged with English ivy and white baby's breath in the hand-cut crystal vase the princess had appropriated from the palace crystal collection.

Her eyes lingered on the velvety red petals, and she sighed—as damsels always do—and imagined her dramatic rescue from the clutches of the Royal Code, the king's high-powered shaking finger, and the queen's scrutinizing eyes. One day true love would be hers, and all would be right with the world.

She reached over and wound the key of her music box. "Someday My Prince Will Come" began to play. She took a flower in her hand, pulled it from the bouquet, and touched it lightly to her cheek. If only he would hurry, she thought.

PART II

Chapter Four

Prince Charming to the Rescue

ONE sunny spring afternoon, as the princess sat behind a textbook in the Imperial University library memorizing the star formation of the Little Dipper, she was startled by a melodious tenor voice.

"I've come to rescue you from the grips of *Complete Analysis of the Skies* by the illustrious Professor Dull."

Rescue? Did someone say *rescue*? Victoria lifted her gaze and found herself looking into two of the bluest eyes she had ever seen, framed by long black lashes that would be the envy of many a girl.

"I beg your pardon. Were you speaking to me?"

"Yes, Princess," the young man said, bowing gallantly. "Indeed I was."

"How do you know I'm a princess?"

"Because a prince always knows a princess. And since I remember from my undergraduate days what it feels like to be subjected to Professor Dull's explanation of what makes the world go round, I thought you might appreciate hearing mine," he said with a sparkle in his eyes that made her heart go pitter-patter and her knees grow weak.

"And what might your explanation be?" she asked demurely.

"Love. Love makes the world go round," he answered with a smile warm enough to melt an avalanche of snow before it ever hit the ground.

Could this vision of masculinity with broad chest and shoulders and jet black hair possibly be the one she had been waiting for all her life? He seemed to fit all her criteria. He was a prince. He had been courageous to approach her. He was charming and handsome. And although being rescued from dying of boredom was unlike any of the rescues she had ever imagined, it was a rescue of sorts, nonetheless.

"I agree," the princess replied, trying to hide her excitement. "Love *does* make the world go round, although at the moment, my world seems to be revolving around learning the Little Dimpler—I mean Dipper," she said quickly, trying to tear her eyes away from the dimples that punctuated his smile—a smile that broadened at her slip of the tongue.

"I am at your service, Princess," he said, sliding out the chair beside her and lowering himself into the seat.

She soon knew more about the stars in the heavens and had more stars in her eyes than she ever imagined possible.

All the way home Victoria had the feeling that something magical had happened. As she replayed every word, every look that she and the prince had exchanged, a sense of excitement spiraled up in her. It was all she could do to keep from laughing aloud.

Suddenly she was overwhelmed with thoughts of Vicky—poor little, long-forgotten Vicky. Victoria wished she could tell her first and very best friend ever about the prince. She thought about how they would giggle together and hug and dance and sing as they had long ago when something wonderful happened. But could she dare to let Vicky out of the closet? A number of questions whirled around in her mind. What would Vicky be like after so many years? And what about the king and queen? And what if this, and what if that?

Using her usual technique for sorting out such things,

Victoria began compiling a mental list of pros and cons. By the time she reached her bedroom and put down her books, it had been decided. A second big event was to occur that day.

She opened the lid of her hope chest and rummaged through the fine linens and lacy garments, taking care not to crush the Royal Family Map that lay on top. She reached deep. Her fingers soon felt the cold metal of the key to the closet that held Vicky captive.

She slowly moved toward the closet and listened at the door. "Vicky—hello—it's me, Victoria."

She rapped lightly. "Vicky, I'm going to open the door. I have something wonderful to tell you. . . . Vicky, answer me."

She placed the gold key in the lock, turned it, and pulled the door slightly open. All she saw was darkness, and still there wasn't a sound. "Vicky. Where are you?" she asked, pulling the door fully open.

There, crouched on the floor with her arms tightly wrapped over her lowered head, was little Vicky.

"Are you okay? Don't be afraid. It's only me, Victoria."

"Go away and leave me alone," the little girl cried, pulling deeper into the recesses of the closet.

"What's the matter, Vicky? I've come to let you out," Victoria said, stepping inside.

"No, get out of here. I don't wanna come out!"

"What do you mean you don't want to come out? You can't stay in here forever."

"Yes, I can. And I wanna. I'm used to it. Go away."

"I have so much to tell you. Please, don't be afraid. I won't hurt you."

"You already did. Lots of times."

"I never meant to. I'm sorry. I really am. Anyway, everything's different now. It won't happen again."

Vicky whimpered. "I don't believe you."

"I mean it, Vicky. I promise. Cross my heart and hope to die, kiss a lizard in one try—remember?"

"I still don't believe you, and I'm not coming out." She sneaked a furtive glance at Victoria. "But I s'pose you can stay in here for a minute if you really wanna."

"This is silly. Come on. We'll sit on the bed like we used to and—"

"No, I can't."

Victoria knelt beside Vicky and put her arm around the child's shoulders to comfort her. At first they huddled together silently on the floor. Soon they were talking and remembering and crying. Finally Victoria was able to coax her little friend out of the closet.

They sat down on the big canopy bed and continued to talk and remember and cry, soaking the silky bedcovers until they dripped tears onto the floor, as Vicky's tears had done so many years before. And as the dawn crept in, they rejoiced that they were together again and had found their long-awaited prince.

♥   ♥

The next morning, at Vicky's urging, Victoria retold the story of meeting the prince, while busily going through her wardrobe closet, garment by garment, searching for exactly the right outfit.

"He sounds wonderful, and I really wanna meet him," Vicky said. "But—what if he doesn't like me? What if he even hates me like the king and queen? Then I'll make trouble for you, and you'll lock me up again and—"

"We'll figure out something, Vicky, but not today. It's too soon to take any chances. Okay?"

Victoria and the prince met as planned, under the big oak tree outside Professor Dull's classroom. The years of practicing batting her eyelashes coyly and sighing demurely proved to have been well spent. Victoria played her role admirably.

To know the prince was to love him. And Victoria wasn't the only one to find it so. Everyone who knew him agreed. Coeds from freshmen to graduate students affectionately called him Prince Charming. Never had the princess known anyone so deserving of such a reputation as he. Many a lady tried to gain the prince's favor, but he fancied only Victoria. He loved her gentle manner and delicate constitution. He admired her wit and was challenged by her intellect. When she was with him, she felt beautiful, special, self-assured, and protected.

One day Victoria invited the prince to the palace to meet the king and queen, who were glad that she had found a suitable prospective mate. It especially pleased them that he was working toward a doctoral degree in inter-kingdom diplomacy. His twinkling eyes and the warmth of his smile permeated the palace. He told jokes that were funnier than those of the court jester, and the entire palace staff was quite taken with him.

In the months that followed, Victoria gradually let the prince get to know Vicky. It was nerve-racking at first, not knowing how he would react. But as it turned out, Victoria's and Vicky's concerns were unwarranted. The more the prince saw of Vicky, the better he liked her. In fact, he reveled in her sensitivity to everyone and everything around her. He shared in her dreams and even enjoyed her singing.

The prince and princess played and laughed and talked and loved. And they studied and studied. When they were apart, the days were endlessly long. When they were together, the days were never long enough. The very June afternoon the princess graduated, the prince won her heart forever. She agreed to become his wife.

A few days before the wedding the princess excitedly began to pack. She would, of course, take her hope chest to the new palace she would soon share with her prince. That was an easy decision. The chest had been lying in wait for years for this very event.

She flipped through the garments hanging in her closet, deciding which to take and which to give to the underprivileged.

As she sat at her dressing table sorting out the drawers, she pondered the Royal Code hanging on the wall before her. No need to take that along, she thought. She had *become* it.

"*I* haven't," Vicky said, bubbling with joy.

"Haven't *what*?"

"Haven't become the Royal Code—like you. But it doesn't matter anyway 'cause the prince loves me the way I am."

"Yes, and what a relief that is. But remember, Vicky, you still need to work on it—just in case."

After carefully wrapping her perfume bottles one by one in tissue paper, the princess picked up her little music box with the elegant couple on top and turned the key. As the sounds of "Someday My Prince Will Come" tinkled out, she looked over at the full-length, brass-framed mirror that still stood in the corner of her bedroom and remembered how beautiful she used to feel when she saw herself in it—so beautiful, in fact, that she was often moved to dance. But that had been when she was very young. After a while the mirror had reflected the same image as the one she saw in her parents' eyes, so she hadn't liked looking at herself in it anymore.

She walked over to the mirror and stared at her reflection there. It was as beautiful as the one reflected from the eyes of her adoring prince. She began to sway to the music, gracefully turning this way and that, swooping down low and reaching up high in a spirited dance that came from somewhere deep inside her. Vicky squealed with pleasure. They were fulfilling their destiny. Their rescue was imminent. Their prince had come. True love would be theirs forever.

♥ ♥

The wedding was glorious, and after an enchanted honeymoon, the happy couple settled down to a new life together in a beautiful palace a short carriage ride away from the princess's parents. The grounds were laced with fruit trees and pink and lavender sweet peas. There was a large rose garden with a white stone bench in the middle, where the prince and princess often sat and reaffirmed their vows to love each other forever.

The prince soon showed himself to be a lot more than charming and handsome. He was also smart and strong and very handy around the palace. He could fix most anything, though he got so busy after a while that sometimes weeks went by before he could make the time. But he always made time to bring the princess fresh-picked, long-stemmed red roses from their garden, which she arranged in hand-cut crystal vases and distributed throughout the palace.

The prince was the light of the princess's life, her reason for being. She lavished him with attention and affection. Every weekday morning she arose early to sit beside him and share a breakfast of hot oatmeal with cinnamon and raisins or buttermilk pancakes with fresh-pressed boysenberry syrup. Then when she thought he wasn't looking, she would secretly print "I love you" in red ink across a napkin and slip it into the sack lunch the royal cook packed for him every day. With a hug and a kiss and a "Have a wonderful day, sweetheart," she would send him off to work at the Royal Embassy.

Life with the prince was everything the princess had ever hoped it would be, and more. She adored being on his arm at diplomatic functions, where she wore the most fashionable gowns. When their friends gathered, he was always the life of the party. Everyone raved about his famous "Childhood Life at the Palace" routine, and they often requested it.

"I always thought my parents wanted me," he would say, "even when they were very busy out kinging and queening. That is, until one day I came home from school and found they had moved!"

This would elicit a round of snickers and chuckles. Then at precisely the right moment, he would add, "And they hadn't even left a forwarding address!"

At this the room would explode with hearty laughter that carried the prince into his next, even funnier, childhood revelation. So funny was he that in private the princess began to teasingly call him Dr. Chuckle.

Damsels from far and near, other princesses, and occasionally even a duchess would ask, "Is the prince like that all the time?" They would say such things as "Your house must be filled with happiness and laughter." And "What a joy he is. How lucky you are to be his wife."

When the royal couple returned home, the charming Dr. Chuckle would wrap his arms around his wife, enveloping her in a blanket of love. "Oh, my darling princess, you truly are a beauty," he would say, and she could feel his chest puff up with pride as he squeezed her against him.

On Sundays the prince and princess usually dined with the king and queen, who soon grew to love the prince as the son they had never had. The prince discussed matters of state with the king, while the princess and queen supervised the preparation of supper. The four attended musical concerts together and went to the Official Kingdom

Olympian Games at Nobility Stadium. On occasion they vacationed together at Lake Relaxaçion.

The princess's responsibilities were many. She fulfilled them all with precision and grace, and still had time to fill the palace with song and laughter and to plan interesting new activities, such as taking archery lessons.

But at their first Sunday morning lesson, it became apparent that there was a problem. Although the princess tried with every ounce of her strength, she simply could not pull the bowstring back far enough to shoot the arrow more than a few yards. Vicky was mortified.

"I'm never, ever going back to that archery range again," the princess announced to the prince on their carriage ride home.

"You didn't do so badly for your first time, Princess." He playfully squeezed her biceps. "If you keep trying, maybe you'll be able to build up these pretty little arms."

Vivid memories of striking out at softball bubbled up in her mind. "They used to call me the 'Third Out,'" she said, feeling as humiliated as she had when she was in school. "I think I had better stick to things I'm good at."

"Fortunately, you're good at many things that are much more important than either softball or archery," the prince replied, raising his eyebrows playfully and giving her a mischievous smile.

The princess smiled unenthusiastically and tried not to think about what once was, but the first recollection triggered another. "And they called me Icky Picky Princess and Miss Perfect," she said, lowering her head.

He took her chin in his hand and raised her face to his. "Those days are over. I love you exactly the way you are."

She knew it was true, for she could see her reflection in his eyes, and it was still beautiful.

When they got back to the palace, the princess curled up on the sofa and began to read the comics in the

Kingdom Times. The king had read them to her as a child, and she had liked them ever since.

The prince was thumbing through the calendar section. "Here's something you'd be good at, Princess," he said. "A local performing arts troupe is holding auditions for *Cinderella.* Let's see—uh—to be performed in royal schools and senior subject centers throughout the kingdom."

"Mmm, well, I don't know."

"I think you should do it, Princess. You're a shoo-in—get it?" he said, his warm, familiar smile widening into a grin that brought out his dimples.

"Do you really think if I tried out, I might get a part?"

"Your voice draws birds from the trees to gather around and sing in harmony with you. And surely there is none fairer than thee. Does that answer your question?"

"Why, Dr. Chuckle sir," said the princess, coyly batting her eyelashes, "I do believe you have your fairy tales mixed up. It is *Snow White,* not *Cinderella,* who is the fairest of them all."

"No, Princess. *You* are the one who is the fairest of them all."

♥ ♥

The princess's audition won her the lead role. On opening night the auditorium at her first alma mater—the Royal Elementary Academy of Excellence—was packed. The prince sat first row center next to the king and queen.

Although Vicky was so nervous that the princess's knees were shaking as she walked onstage, she played a superb Cinderella and received a rousing standing ovation. As she took her last bow, the prince reached up and handed her a dozen of the most beautiful long-stemmed red roses she had ever seen.

Later, backstage, the reviewer from the *Kingdom Times*

told the princess that she had a voice like an angel and that she really should consider auditioning for a professional role at the Grand Regal Theater.

The king and queen flitted from one compliment to another, responding with such comments as "Thank you. Even as a small child, she showed much talent in song and dance." And "She's quite clever and witty as well." And "She comes by it rightly. I was quite talented as a child myself, you know."

The producer was exuberant. "From the moment I saw you onstage at the first rehearsal, I knew your performance would be exceptional," he said. Then he presented her with a miniature pair of glass slippers, etched with her initials.

But the highlight of the princess's evening was seeing the sparkle in the prince's eyes and knowing they sparkled for her. They sparkled so brightly, they lit up the darkness as the couple walked hand in hand to their carriage. He squeezed her hand gently—his special way of silently saying "I love you." All was right with the world.

Chapter Five

Dr. Chuckle and Mr. Hide

THE princess was deep in thought when the prince, taking a break from a pile of work he had brought home from the embassy, asked what was on her pretty little mind.

"I was just imagining what would happen if I were to follow the reviewer's advice and audition for a part at the Grand Regal Theater."

"You would undoubtedly get it," the prince said matter-of-factly. "Then you'd be cast in bigger and bigger parts and become a famous performer."

The princess smiled. "I haven't even auditioned yet, and you've already made me a star."

"It would only be a matter of time. I can see it all now," he said, sitting tall and sweeping his hand grandly in front of him. "Your name spelled out on the billboard in gigantic letters. A standing-room-only crowd— It's a smash hit!" he belted out, sounding like a sportscaster announcing a home run.

Then, suddenly the prince grew quiet. He nervously toyed with the edges of the papers stacked in front of him. "From then on," he said at last, "you would be in such demand you wouldn't have time for me. And you'd have scores of new theatrical friends I'd have nothing in common—"

"*Scores* of theatrical friends. Very witty, Dr. Chuckle,"

she said, trying to tease him out of his surprising melancholy.

He slumped forward, and his voice dropped low. "It would probably mean the end of our marriage."

"That's ridiculous! I can't believe you would say such a thing!"

"I know you, Princess. I know what you're capable of better than you do— It would happen, believe me. And I love you far too much to risk losing you. I don't want you to do it. Forget about performing at the Grand Regal Theater or anywhere else—please. If you want to do something, maybe it's a good time for us to start a family."

The princess was both astonished and disappointed. But her first priority was the prince. She decided right then and there to give up the idea of ever again appearing onstage.

Vicky, however, had no intention of giving up. "This whole thing is stupid," she said after the prince left the room. "You're not gonna listen to him, are you?"

"Yes, actually I am," Victoria answered.

"But you can't! That's not fair. You know how I love to sing and dance. Maybe we really *could* be famous."

"Oh, Vicky. You heard what the prince said. And you promised to stop dreaming of things that probably won't ever happen."

"But it *could* happen! I 'member how the king said our singing was for the birds and the queen said our dancing was humil-er-ating. But now, after *Cinderella*—everyone loved us!"

"I know, Vicky," Victoria said sympathetically. "But the prince loves us more. And we love him. You wouldn't want to do anything to make him unhappy or to make us lose him, would you?"

"Well—I guess that'd be even worse than not getting to be a famous star," she grumbled, and didn't mention it again.

The more Victoria thought about having a baby, the better she liked the idea. And so the prince and princess tried and tried and hoped and hoped, but month after month they were disappointed.

Several winters in a row were particularly cold, and virulent flus thrived and spread throughout the kingdom. The princess frequently became ill. The prince would bring home chicken soup for her from the embassy commissary and serve it to her in bed. Then he would sit with her and tell her the latest news from Kingdom Hill.

As time went on, the prince began to complain that his job at the embassy was too stressful and his fellow diplomats were stuffy and boring. He said there were times he was sorry he had ever been born a prince. He would have been happier being a blacksmith. The princess was both concerned and disappointed. She had always thought that with all his potential and charm, he was sure to rise to the top of the diplomatic service.

After a while the prince's collection of grievances grew so large that he was appointed president of the Royal Grievance Committee—which wasn't exactly what the princess had had in mind for him—but he soon tired of this new responsibility. As a matter of fact, he was tired of having *any* responsibilities. He didn't even want the princess to ask him to fix things around the palace anymore. Still, he was as loving and charming as ever, and much funnier. He spent more and more time performing his repertoire of jokes—including his "Childhood Life at the Palace" routine—for anyone within earshot, and he thrived on the rave reviews. Dr. Chuckle was indeed in rare form.

The princess loved Dr. Chuckle, heart and soul. She tried harder than ever to show him how much, but the prince said it was not enough. He accused her of not loving him as much as he loved her. She tried every way she could think of to prove her love—including getting advice from the Royal Fertility Clinic—but the more love she gave, the more he seemed to need.

Late one afternoon the princess was preparing one of her specialties for supper—Broccoli Fettuccine with Pistachio Pesto Sauce. She dismissed the cook early. She loved to cook the evening meal herself—especially when a guest was coming. She danced around the kitchen, her voice ringing out in song:

> I love my prince,
> And he loves me.
> We'll be so happy
> When we are three.

Birds from the trees flew in through her kitchen windows to gather around and sing in harmony with her. Everything was going fine until the prince arrived home with his guest earlier than expected.

"Victoria, what on earth is going on here!" he shouted.

The princess froze. She wrinkled her nose, shrugged her shoulders, and gave him a halfhearted smile. "Uh—I'm making one of your favorite suppers?" she answered tentatively, brushing pistachio crumbs from the feet of a squirming bluebird that had slightly misjudged its landing.

The prince gave her a look that chilled her to the bone. Without a word, he quickly ushered the visiting dignitary out of the kitchen through the white louvered swinging doors.

Although she immediately shooed out the birds, straightened her apron, fluffed her hair, and composed herself—and in spite of the fact that her broccoli fettuccine was quite a hit—the prince was still angry with her when his guest left.

"That undignified display was humiliating, Victoria! Completely unbefitting a princess. You made a spectacle of yourself. Won't you ever grow up?"

Vicky started moaning loudly, "Oh, no! First the king and queen, then you, Victoria, and now the prince. I thought he loved me."

The princess lowered her head to avoid having to see her reflection in the prince's eyes.

Later that night he came into the bedroom where the dismayed princess was brushing her hair in preparation for bed. He took a single red rose from the arrangement on her dressing table and on bended knee extended it up to her.

"I'm so sorry, Princess, for saying such terrible things. I had a miserable day at the embassy. I didn't mean to take it out on you. Please accept this gift as a token of my love and know that this will never happen again," he said, his face breaking into a smile that showed his dimples. His eyes twinkled the twinkle that still made her heart go pitter-patter and her knees grow weak.

Well, she thought, his intentions were certainly pure enough. Then he took her in his arms, and all was forgiven and forgotten.

♥ ♥

The princess built quite a reputation as a fine chef of natural gourmet foods. Friends and dinner guests clamored for her recipes, making the prince very proud.

One evening after dining at their palace, the wife of the commissioner of Inter-kingdom Transportation raved about the meal and suggested that the princess compile her much sought-after recipes into a book. The prince thought it was a splendid idea.

"I don't know how to write a book," the princess said later after their guests had left. "And even if I could figure out how to do it, it probably wouldn't get published, anyway."

"Oh, Princess. You always doubt that you can do things you've never done before. Of course you can do it."

And so he encouraged her. He bought her new quills and parchment upon which to record her culinary creations. He tasted and rated new recipes and praised her efforts.

After several months of working on the book, the princess was sitting at her kitchen desk one sunny afternoon, her quill gliding across the parchment as she recorded directions for assembling her Creamy Lemon-Herb Vegetable Soufflé. All at once she felt a chill run down the entire length of her body as an eerie breeze swirled through the room. She looked up and saw the prince. His piercing, icy glare bore into her.

"You care more about that miserable book than you do about me," he said, his face contorting into an angry scowl. "You didn't even look up when I came in!"

The princess sat there for a moment, stunned. "I-I was working on this. I guess I didn't hear you."

"That's nothing new. You *never* pay attention to me anymore. Every time I look at you, you're either cooking or writing something down."

"I-I'm sorry. I thought you *wanted* me to write this book," the princess said, beginning to shake inside.

"What makes you think it'll be good enough for anyone to publish, anyway?"

"*You* made me think it. I thought you were proud of me."

"Proud? Of what?" the prince snarled. "A wife who's always dreaming of things that probably won't ever happen? A wife who doesn't love her husband enough to be there when he needs her?"

"I *am* there when you need me. And I *do* love you. I love you heart and soul. I always have. You *know* that. Didn't I instruct the royal cook to prepare wonderful breakfasts of hot oatmeal with cinnamon and raisins or

buttermilk pancakes with fresh-pressed boysenberry syrup
for you, and don't I get up early every day to sit and eat
them with you?" she asked, her voice beginning to rise.
"Don't I always put love notes in your lunches and massage
your neck and shoulders when you come home tense from
a hard day at the embassy? Haven't I told you time and
again how charming and handsome and wonderful you are?
Aren't I the best audience you ever had for your jokes and
stories? Don't I entertain your friends, keep the palace
running smoothly, and put red roses all around to remind us
of our special love? Don't I sit on the stone bench in the
rose garden with you and—"

"That's enough, Victoria! I *hate* it when you get into
these endless explanations." He turned and stormed out of
the room.

The princess felt as if a pigeon-driven butter churner
were running at high speed in her stomach. Her chest
tightened like a vise, and her head began to ache as the
sound of Vicky's hysterical voice blasted in her ears, "He
hates us! He hates us!"

Later, as the princess lay crying into her pillow on
their big brass bed, the prince came in and sat down beside
her. He told her over and over again how sorry he was,
how he hadn't meant the things he had said to her, and how
the last thing in the world he would ever want to do was to
hurt her. He told her how much he loved her and promised
that nothing like that would ever happen again.

"That's what you said last time," she said, her voice
muffled by the pillow. "What's the matter with you?"

"I don't know, Princess. Something comes over me. I
can't explain it."

She lifted her head. "What could it be?"

"I wish I knew. This power comes over me, and I hear
myself saying terrible things. I can't believe they're coming
out of my own mouth."

"Well, it certainly isn't my Dr. Chuckle saying them. That's for sure," she said, sniffling.

"No. He hides."

"Hides . . . hmm . . . that reminds me of something. A story I once heard about a horrible monster named Mr. Hyde," she said, sitting up and trying to clear her head. "Now let's see, how did that go? Yes, I remember. Sometimes this Mr. Hyde took over a man named Dr. Jekyll and made him do dreadful things— Why, that's exactly what happens to you!" she said, wide-eyed. "Dr. Chuckle becomes Mr. Hide!"

"Do you really think so? How could that be?" the prince asked.

"I don't know. It must be a spell or something."

"That's it! That's it! Someone has cast an evil spell on me."

"Well, I *have* noticed an eerie breeze swirl through the room right before the twinkle in your eyes turns into an icy glare."

"Princess, you have to help me, please," the prince begged, desperately clutching the princess's shoulders.

"Oh, my darling. Of course I'll help you," she said, throwing her arms around the prince and pulling him against her. "Haven't I vowed to love you and cherish you in good times and bad, in sickness and in health, till death do us part? Try not to worry. We'll figure this out together—somehow."

Chapter Six

You Always Crush the Sweetest Rose

THE day that Kingdom Publishing brought out the *Royal Family Natural Gourmet Recipe Book,* the prince had the princess autograph dozens of copies, which he proudly gave to everyone at the embassy and to all his fellow members of the Royal Grievance Committee. He also gave copies to his squire, his coachman, and the ice delivery man. But the prince soon lost his enthusiasm, having grown tired of hanging around bookstores at autograph-signing parties watching people fuss over the princess. What bothered him even more was that at social gatherings they attended, people paid so much attention to the princess that there was hardly any time left for him to tell his jokes or perform his "Childhood Life at the Palace" routine.

The glory was bittersweet for the princess as she was extremely worried about the prince. Figuring out how to help him was her first priority. First she called Imperial University and spoke to the head of the Department of Supernatural Powers. He said he'd get back to her. Then she went to the Kingdom Public Library and checked out everything she could find on spells and witchcraft, hoping to find an antidote. The prince asked her to do the research, saying he was too absorbed in problems at the embassy to concentrate on anything else. But before she had a chance to finish reading the material she had collected, it happened again. Mr. Hide returned—much sooner than the time before.

At first the spell had come over the prince only once in a great while and lasted for only a few minutes. But as time went on, it appeared more often and lasted for hours or days. By the time Mr. Hide left, the princess felt as if she had been trampled by a horse gone berserk. And each time, it took her longer to get over it.

Her sweet, funny Dr. Chuckle always showed up afterward with that familiar, irresistible twinkle in his eyes. He apologized profusely and begged for one more chance, swearing that it would never happen again. But it *did* happen again . . . and again . . . and again.

The princess grew very nervous, never knowing who would arise with her in the morning or who would come home to her at night—Dr. Chuckle or Mr. Hide. Each time Mr. Hide appeared, he seemed meaner than the time before. He was as critical as Dr. Chuckle was accepting, as hurtful as Dr. Chuckle was kind, as hateful as Dr. Chuckle was loving. He took pleasure in causing her pain—and he was good at it. He knew all the things the princess had told the prince in confidence—all her private thoughts and fears and dreams—and he became expert at using them to hurt her.

Knowing that the prince was good, through and through, and that he couldn't help what he said and did while under the influence of the evil spell, the princess tried harder than ever to find a way to free him. She cut out articles from back issues of the *Kingdom Journal of Mysticism,* which she had ordered sent to the palace. She underlined the important parts in red so that reading them wouldn't take up too much of the prince's valuable time, and she left them on the kitchen table where he was sure to see them. Still, the information was sketchy at best.

The princess decided she needed a carefully thought-out plan. She sat down with quill in hand and made a list of every way she could think of to help the prince get rid of the evil spell. After all, she thought, every problem had a solution. She simply had to find it, that was all. Then she set about trying out each item on her list, one at a time.

First she suggested to the prince that he seek counsel from a professional. Perhaps the royal director of prayer, who was eminently qualified to deal with evil doings. Or the court magician, who was expert at making things disappear. The prince vetoed both. Thinking he might be more comfortable with someone he didn't know, she suggested the astrologer from across the kingdom, who she heard had excellent credentials. The prince replied that he had no intention of discussing his problem with some stranger who probably couldn't help him anyway.

"Then you have to fight harder not to let the spell take over," the princess told him resolutely.

"I *have* been trying, Princess. I've been trying very hard. But the spell is so powerful. Right when I think I'm getting better, Mr. Hide shows up—and there isn't anything I can do to stop him." The prince sounded desperate.

"You've always been so courageous, my prince. Surely you're not going to let some old evil spell win out over you."

"I can't do it without your help. You're much better at these things than I am. If you love me, really love me, you'll find a way to get rid of the spell."

The next time Mr. Hide showed up, the princess tried the second item on her list—appealing to him to stop tormenting her. But that didn't work. So she went on to the next item—threatening to run away if he kept coming back. That didn't work either.

The princess had no intention of giving up, regardless of whether or not the prince did. She would be brave and strong enough for them both, if necessary. She had to be.

The next time Mr. Hide appeared, she stood eye-to-eye and toe-to-toe with him.

"I'll fight you to the death to get my Dr. Chuckle back for good," she said in the most forceful voice she could muster up.

Mr. Hide threw back his head and laughed. *"You?* Fight *me* to the death? Fragile, weak little thing that you are. Afraid of your own shadow. Can't even pull back the string on a bow. Sick every time a cool breeze blows. I'm shaking in my boots, Princess," he boomed.

He might not have been shaking, but *she* certainly was. And her stomach was churning, her chest was so tight that she could barely breathe, and her temples began to throb as Vicky's cries of anguish exploded in her head.

The princess grew weary and had run out of things to try. So when Mr. Hide appeared the next time, Victoria told Vicky not to listen, that the prince didn't mean what he was saying, that he couldn't help the things Mr. Hide said and did.

The princess often sat and gazed wistfully at her white wooden hope chest with the clusters of hand-carved roses at the corners and hoped as hard as she could . . . and remembered . . . and waited. After a while, she was spending more time *waiting* for her Prince Charming than *being with* him.

It became an effort for her to get through each day. There was so much confusion—with Victoria and Vicky and Dr. Chuckle and Mr. Hide coming and going, each saying that the others were mixed up about what was going on—that the princess could no longer be sure of what she was seeing and hearing and thinking and feeling. And she was weak from all the worrying, shaking, stomach churning, chest tightening, head aching, and crying, as well as from the heart-wrenching discussions with Dr. Chuckle, nightmarish encounters with Mr. Hide, and continuous efforts to calm down Vicky.

She wasn't getting much sleep either—especially the nights Mr. Hide was there. Night after night he said something mean or accused her of something upsetting right before they fell asleep. Then he would turn over and fall immediately into a deep slumber so she didn't have a chance to say anything at all. Why he said it, whether he meant it, whether it was true, what she could have said, would have said, wanted to say, all clanged around in her mind for hours.

The longer she lay there, the more intense became the shaking, churning, tightening, and aching. What made matters worse was that she was afraid to move—even to scratch an itch—because Mr. Hide would abruptly awaken, yelling terrible things at her and accusing her of trying to annoy him on purpose. Eventually she would escape into a fitful sleep, hoping and praying that it would be Dr. Chuckle who awoke beside her in the morning.

When Mr. Hide was with her, she worried about how long it was going to take for him to go away. When Dr. Chuckle was with her, she worried about how long he would stay. When she was alone, she worried about which of them would show up next, and she tried to figure out how to get the shaking, churning, tightening, and aching to stop. After a while she stopped trying, as she forgot what it felt like to be calm.

When she thought she couldn't stand the craziness for one more minute, Dr. Chuckle would usually come home, crying buckets of tears and saying he was sorry. He would tell her that Mr. Hide said things to hurt her even though they weren't true. That she was sweet and good and special and that he was lucky to have her as his wife. He would tell her he was getting better—that she was only imagining things were getting worse. And he would say that he'd try harder and that everything would soon be as wonderful as it used to be.

She savored every word and believed with all her heart. The sparkle in his eyes would make her heart go pitter-patter and her knees grow weak. She would melt into his arms and say, "My darling Prince Charming, my precious Dr. Chuckle, thank heavens you're back." And the memory of Mr. Hide's icy glare would drift from her mind as if it had never existed.

♥ ♥

The princess was enjoying a rare happy moment as sunlight streamed through the kitchen window and danced on the crystal vases she was emptying in preparation for the fresh flowers the prince had gone out in the garden to pick. She glanced at the note from the prince she had tacked on the wall that very morning after discovering it on the kitchen counter.

> Roses are red,
> Violets are blue.
> The best wife in the kingdom
> Is you, Princess, you.

Suddenly the back door banged open, and in burst the prince. He threw down a large handful of roses on the drainboard in front of her. Red petals flew into the sink and onto the floor.

"Enjoy these, Princess. They're the last ones you'll ever get from me! I suggest you get used to picking them yourself!"

The princess looked at him in disbelief. "What? What are you talking about?"

"I pricked my finger on a thorn, and that's when I realized who cast this evil spell on me."

"That's wonderful! Who was it?"

"As if you didn't already know!" the prince shouted. "It's *you*, Princess. You!" he said, pointing an accusing finger at her.

"What? *Me?* The one who's been trying to help you? The one who—"

"Don't start all that again. It won't get you out of this."

"Out of *what*? I didn't do anything."

"Is that right?" he said angrily. "Well, the spell only comes over me when I'm with you. It never happens with anyone else. So what do you think of *that*, Miss Perfect, Icky Picky Princess? It's your fault! All this time, *you've* been the one doing this to me!" he shouted, deliberately crushing a fallen rose petal beneath his boot.

She felt as if she had been stabbed in the heart. "I don't even know *how* to cast a spell," she barely managed to say, wondering if it could possibly be true.

"It doesn't matter. I know it's your fault."

The princess followed the prince, pleading with him to listen, as he burst out of the kitchen, banging the louvered doors out of his way. One door nearly knocked the princess off her feet as she rushed through behind him.

"I have to get out of here!" he yelled, storming through the palace. Then out the entry doors he flew, calling for his carriage.

The princess tore after him. As she ran out the front doors of the palace, she saw the prince standing next to his carriage, slamming his fist against the door. He was muttering something she couldn't understand—and didn't think she wanted to.

She stopped abruptly, then cautiously stepped toward him. "Are you all right?" she asked. "What happened to you?"

"*You* happened to me," he shouted. "It's your fault!"

The coachman, who was standing silently by, looked

quizzically at the princess and shrugged his shoulders.

"*My* fault? What did *I* do?" she asked the prince.

"That's it. Play dumb. For someone who's supposed to be smart, you sure can't figure out much for yourself, can you? Well, answer me. Can you?"

The princess's throat went dry. She couldn't get a word out.

"Never mind, O Brilliant One. I'll tell you. I smacked my leg getting into the carriage."

"That's *my* fault?" she asked meekly, afraid of making him angrier.

The prince limped over to her, shaking his fist in the air. "If I wasn't so furious with you, I wouldn't have had to get out of here so fast. And I wouldn't have been thinking about how you've betrayed me instead of paying attention to what I'm doing," he shouted, his face turning bright red. "If not for you, I never would've gotten hurt!"

Wishing she could just disappear, the princess lowered her head and stared at the ground in front of her, careful to avoid his eyes.

His icy stare and angry voice continued to pummel her. "Look at me when I talk to you, Victoria!" he demanded.

She looked up with big frightened eyes. There, behind the icy glare, was her reflection showing exactly what was wrong with her. The princess blinked back her tears.

The prince shook his fist vigorously in front of her nose, the veins on the side of his neck standing out as his voice thundered in her ears. "You're much too sensitive, Victoria! Too delicate. Can't even beget a child!" His voice rose higher. "What's the matter with you? Why can't you be like other royal wives!" Then he threw up his hands in frustration. "What did I ever do to deserve this?"

Vicky started making such loud noises to shut out his voice that the princess's head began to pound. She turned and raced back into the palace, where she dashed into the sitting room and slammed the door.

"What are we gonna do now?" Vicky sniffled.

"I don't know," Victoria answered, sinking into the gold-fringed sofa. "Let me think."

"But you have to know!"

"Vicky, please. Keep quiet for a few minutes so I can think."

Vicky waited. Then, when she couldn't stand to hear even one more rhythmic ticktock of the clock on the mantel, she blurted out what had long been on her mind. "Maybe—maybe the evil spell *is* our fault. Maybe *everything* is our fault."

"Not you, too! How can you say such a thing?"

"I just feel it. Anyway, the prince wouldn't lie to us. He's Prince Charming. Everybody says so."

"You can't always believe what everybody says, Vicky. And I'm not so sure anymore about the prince not lying to us."

"But what if he's right?" Vicky asked. "What if he's 'llergic to us or something? Or what if the stuff we say and do really does make the spell come over him, like he says?"

"Oh, Vicky. For heaven's sake!"

"It only comes over him when he's with us. No one else's ever even met Mr. Hide. 'Cept the coachman, just now."

That seemed true enough, so Victoria tried and tried to think of what they might have done to make the evil spell come over the prince, but she couldn't come up with a single thing. She guessed they must be doing lots of wrong things to make so many bad things happen, but she had a lot of trouble figuring out what.

"I don't know what to think anymore, Vicky," Victoria said. "I'm so tired. So very tired."

"You're the one who's good at figuring things out. You have to think of something."

Vicky waited nervously as Victoria agonized over the problem.

"Maybe there's some truth in what you say, Vicky. We surely can't afford to take a chance. I guess we'll have to try harder not to do or say or think anything that might bring on the evil spell."

"But how can we try harder?"

"We'll have to be good. Better than good. Perfect, in fact."

"I can't do it. I tried with the king and queen, 'member? I can't do any better than I already am."

"Well, I think you had better try. And this time I hope you can do it, or the prince may leave us."

♥ ♥

So the princess tried every day in every way to be perfect enough not to bring on the evil spell. But what brought it on one day was not the same as what brought it on another. Nevertheless, Vicky—who had never gotten over not being good enough to be loved by the king and queen and still had occasional nightmares about being separated from Victoria all the time she had been imprisoned in the closet—wasn't taking any chances with the prince. She spent every waking moment trying so hard to be good, to be better than good, to be perfect in fact, that she ran Victoria ragged.

Vicky was no longer satisfied that the palace maids were doing a good enough job, so she insisted that Victoria go around and reclean things. And although the princess, time and time again, had entertained the prince's dignitary friends with skill and flair, Vicky now worried and became anxious every time a gala event was being planned. She insisted that Victoria make all the food herself, from scratch, and that every plate be garnished with hand-curled butter rosebuds, and that carrots and radishes be cut into perfect corkscrews. The cook tried to help, but Vicky wouldn't let her. By the time the guests arrived, Victoria was too tired to enjoy the evening.

When Victoria had a decision to make, no matter how small, Vicky would put herself in charge of making sure they wouldn't make a mistake. So afraid was Vicky of making the wrong choice that she would convince Victoria to write a note asking the queen what to do—since she was practically always right—and have one of the maids ride it over on horseback and wait for an answer. But the maids spent so much time riding back and forth that many days they didn't have time to do the laundry or ironing—so Victoria had to do it.

The situation was even worse when the princess had to decide how to vote on an issue in her capacity as member-in-good-standing of the prestigious Sovereign Committee for the Underprivileged. Victoria would make a list of the pros and cons, and then, precisely when she thought she knew how to vote, Vicky would try to sway her. If she changed her mind and agreed with Vicky, her little friend would try to sway her back the other way. Sometimes the princess simply sat there, confused and flustered, as the other eleven committee members waited impatiently for her decision.

But none of the princess's efforts made any difference as far as Mr. Hide was concerned. He walked around with his scowl and icy glare, looking for something to get angry about. When there was nothing, he invented something.

The expression on the princess's face was often enough to make him fly into a rage. But she couldn't do anything to prevent it because she never knew which expression would set him off. Sometimes he performed his mind-reading feat and became furious with her for what he said she was thinking. When the princess tried to tell him that she wasn't thinking what he thought she was, he accused her of denying the truth. "I know better than you do what's in that scheming little head of yours," he would say.

Convinced that she couldn't be perfect enough to stop Mr. Hide, Vicky became more miserable every day, making Victoria more miserable, too.

"I am what I am," Vicky mumbled one day, so quietly that Victoria had to strain to hear her. "And what I am isn't good enough. You'll never get along with him as long as I'm around. Maybe I should run away and never come back."

Victoria sat silently, wondering if Vicky could possibly be right.

After that, Vicky ordered herself into the bedroom closet. She marched in and slammed the door shut behind her. She sat on the floor in the dark, huddled up in the back corner, and tried to muffle the sound of her whimpering. But it didn't help—the prince's attitude grew worse and worse.

Night after night the princess lay awake staring into the shadows of the bedroom as teardrops rolled past her temples and dampened her hair. But she never wiped them away. She was too afraid of disturbing the volatile stranger who slept beside her.

Sometimes she would watch him slumbering peacefully. She saw the same courageous, charming, handsome prince she had fallen in love with—and still loved. She longed to run her fingers through the jet black hair she knew so well and snuggle into the strong, comforting arms that so many times had warmed her heart and soul. He lay right there, so near and yet so far. Memories of him tugged at her heartstrings. Many times she desperately longed for her prince, even as he lay right beside her.

One morning the princess awakened late from a

restless sleep and dragged herself out of bed. Her stomach ached from all the churning, and the chest tightening had given her a bad cough. Dr. Chuckle had never before stayed away for so long. She didn't know how much longer she could go on without him.

"Where is Dr. Chuckle?" she asked Mr. Hide, who was already dressing. "I haven't seen him in weeks."

"He's gone."

"He can't be! I know he's in there somewhere. He wouldn't ever leave me. He vowed to love and cherish me, in good times and in bad, in sickness and in health, till—"

"Till death do you part. Well, guess what, Princess—he's dead. The prince you knew has been dead for a long time. So you might as well stop wishing and waiting and hoping and crying. He's dead, and he's never coming back."

"I know you're in there, my precious prince," she said with a lump in her throat so big that her voice could barely squeeze by it. She peered deep into his eyes—past the icy glare, past her reflection—and there, right where she knew it would be, was a faint little twinkle. The twinkle that she knew was for her.

An ocean of tears rose from her very soul and nearly drowned her in sorrow. She sobbed, and she remembered how for years she had dreamed of her fairy-tale life with her Prince Charming. And this was what it had come to. She sobbed harder. Suddenly she longed for the comfort of her old childhood room, her fluffy pink quilt and piles of downy pillows. Perhaps if she went back home for a visit, she could decide in peace what to do.

But Vicky hated the idea. "I'm not going anywhere," she wailed as Victoria packed a few things in her paisley overnight bag. "I'd rather die than leave the prince. He needs me, and I need him."

"We're only going there to rest and think about what

to do. No one said anything about leaving the prince."

"Well—I can't stay here alone with Mr. Hide, that's for sure. I s'pose I'll have to go with you. But promise we'll come back. Say, 'Cross my heart and hope to die, kiss—'"

"Cross my heart and hope to die. Now come on, Vicky. Let's go."

Chapter Seven

A Meeting of Minds and Hearts

ON the carriage ride to her parents' palace, the princess tried to think up an excuse to tell the king and queen for showing up unannounced and alone with her paisley overnight bag in hand. A number of possibilities came to mind, but by the time she arrived, she had decided to tell them about the prince and the evil spell. She had kept the secret as long as she possibly could.

"Where is the queen?" the princess asked the servant who answered the door.

"In the library, I believe, Princess."

"Please see that this is put in my old bedroom," she said, handing him her bag.

"Why, Princess," the king said, walking toward her from the other end of the foyer. "I thought I heard your voice. What a surprise!"

The princess wrapped her arms around her father. Her head lingered on his shoulder.

"Was that an overnight bag you sent upstairs?" he asked. "Are you planning to stay?"

"For a couple of days, if I may."

"Of course, Princess, but—"

"I need to talk to you and Mother."

"Are you all right? You don't look—"

"Please, Father. It'll be easier if I talk to you both at the same time."

"I don't like the sound of this, Victoria. I don't like it at all," the king said, putting his arm around her shoulders as they walked silently down the corridor to the library.

"Victoria!" her mother said, getting up from the sofa. "We did not expect you. Is the prince with you?"

"No, Mother. He's not."

"You look tired," the queen said with concern. "Come over here and sit down." Once they were seated on the sofa, the queen observed her daughter carefully. "Are you sick?"

Tears sprang to the princess's eyes, and her whole body seemed to tie itself into a big knot. She struggled to keep her composure.

"What is it, Princess?" the king asked, sitting down in a nearby armchair.

A stream of painful words tumbled from her lips about the terrible evil spell and cruel Mr. Hide. She left out the worst parts because she knew the king and queen loved the prince like a son and she didn't want to hurt them any more than necessary.

"I can hardly believe it's true!" the king exclaimed.

"No wonder you look so sick and tired," the queen said, shaking her head in disbelief.

"I *am* sick and tired, Mother. I'm sick and tired of the prince being angry with me. Of being blamed for everything that goes wrong. Of shaking and of my stomach churning, my chest tightening, and my head hurting. Of wishing and hoping and crying and waiting—and of picking my own roses. . . . And I'm sick and tired of being sick and tired."

"*Our* Prince Charming? How can it be?" the queen questioned. "Why have we never seen any demonstration of this erratic behavior, Victoria?"

"Because it happens only in front of me," the princess answered, holding back her tears.

"Well, then," the king said, "have you considered that

maybe the prince was right in thinking you had a part in causing the evil spell? Why else would it happen only with you? Surely such a thing wouldn't happen all by itself. You must be doing *something*."

Vicky's voice reverberated in Victoria's head. "I knew he'd say that. I knew it! That's what he always said."

"Victoria?—Victoria!" the queen said, raising her voice to jar the princess into attention. "Are you absolutely sure the situation is as bad as you think? Forgive me for saying so, dear, but you have on occasion been known to confuse what is real with what is not."

"I'm not sure of much of anything right now, Mother."

The king stood and began to pace back and forth, his hands clasped behind his back. "I don't understand this. The prince has kept to himself a bit lately—but this!"

"I am so sorry about all this, Victoria," the queen said. "Perhaps it would help if your father and I talked to the prince."

"I doubt if anyone can get through to him. But he has always loved you both, so maybe. . . . " She leaned over into the solace of her mother's lap. "I don't know what to do anymore. I don't know."

That evening the three of them had a quiet supper, and the princess retired early to her old, pink and white bedroom with the big canopy bed. Everything looked exactly as it had when she left to marry the prince. The queen had ordered the palace housekeeping staff to maintain it that way.

The princess ran her hand across the top of her dressing table and straightened the Royal Code of Feelings and Behavior for Princesses that still hung on the wall above. She glanced at the full-length, brass-framed mirror standing in the corner of the room and thought about the beautiful reflection of a little princess she used to see there. She also remembered the reflection that had shown her exactly what was wrong with her. Not wanting to disturb the calm coming over her, she kept her distance from the mirror.

She was so tired that it was an effort to undress. She pulled her blue silk nightgown out of the overnight bag and slipped it over her head, noticing that the color matched her mood. She got into bed and snuggled under the fluffy pink quilts, pulling up a corner of one and rubbing its softness against her cheek. She felt comforted somehow and wearily slipped off to sleep.

♥ ♥

In the morning the princess was awakened by the chirping of birds in the trees outside her bedroom. She was greeted by rays of sunlight streaming across her room. She had slept better than she had in months. Then the painful reality of where she was, and why, struck her like a stray discus at the Official Kingdom Olympian Games. She got out of bed, wrapped herself in her robe, and went to freshen up.

When she returned, there was a tray of buttermilk pancakes with fresh-pressed boysenberry syrup and a cup of hot herbal tea on her night table. She climbed back into bed and pulled the tray onto her lap. It had been a long time since she had been served breakfast in bed.

She thought back to all the other mornings she had had buttermilk pancakes brought to that same room. The same tray had been placed on the same night table. When she had been happy, she had delved into the pancakes with enthusiasm and enjoyed every morsel. When she had been sad, she had mindlessly pushed pieces around the plate until they absorbed so much syrup that they hung limply from the sides of the fork when she finally raised it to her mouth. This was definitely a limp pancake kind of day.

She pushed the tray aside and took the cup of tea to the window seat. As she curled up and looked out at the view she had seen so many times before, the memory of all the dreams she had built and nurtured sitting in that very seat crept into her mind, one by one. Everything seemed so different, she thought, yet so much the same.

At that moment her eyes found their way to the tree that stood alone atop the little hill just beyond the palace gardens. It looked as sad and lonely out there all by itself as it had the day long ago when she had gone out and talked to it, or at least thought she talked to it. That was the day she had met Henry Herbert Hoot, Doctor of the Heart. A solitary tear escaped from the corner of her eye and trickled down her cheek as it had that day long ago. Oh, Doc, she thought. If only I could talk to you now.

The door opened slightly, and the queen poked her head into the room. "How are you feeling today, Victoria?" she asked, stepping inside.

"A little better I guess, Mother. It helps to be here."

"Good," the queen said, joining her on the window seat and drawing her fingers slowly through the princess's hair with long, gentle strokes.

"Remember when you used to sit on my bed at night and do that until I fell asleep?" asked the princess. "And we would talk about the fairy tales and about how my prince would come one day. I was so happy. I wonder if I'll ever be happy like that again."

"Of course you will," the queen replied, giving the princess a reassuring hug. "Now you must get ready to come downstairs. Father and I have summoned the prince, and I expect him momentarily."

♥ ♥

It was a sad prince who greeted the queen and princess

when they entered the library. He leaned forward and kissed the queen lightly on the cheek. "Hello, Mother," he said softly.

He looked at the princess and smiled a half smile that crinkled the corners of his eyes. Without a word he took her hand and squeezed it gently in his special way. He led her to the sofa and sat down beside her. For an instant the princess's eyes met his, and she saw a faint sparkle still flickering there deep inside. She was riveted to her seat, barely able to breathe, feeling nothing but the pounding of her own heart.

The king, who had been observing from an armchair, looked directly at the prince. "Now, what is all this we hear about an evil spell and a Mr. Hide, and about the princess shaking and churning and tightening and hurting and crying and picking her own roses?"

The prince admitted that it was all true and told them everything that he and the princess had done to try and get rid of the spell.

"Through it all she has been my best friend," he said, his voice quivering with emotion. He squeezed the princess's hand again in his special way. "She believed in me even when Mr. Hide was being cruel to her. She was there for me even when I wasn't there for myself."

"The princess says you blame her for the spell," the king said.

"No, Mr. Hide blamed her for it. I always knew it wasn't her fault."

"You must fight this evil spell with all your might, or it will destroy everything you hold most dear," the queen said.

"The spell is much too powerful," the prince replied. "I can't fight it. I haven't the strength. I've tried."

"But you must!" the queen insisted.

"I'm so sorry," the prince said, looking from the queen

to the king and back again. "I love you both so much. I never meant to hurt you like this. And I never wanted to hurt the princess, either. I've loved her from the first moment I saw her, and I can't bear the idea of ever being without her—nor can I bear to go on hurting her this way." The prince's eyes became so filled with tears that when he lowered his head, they dropped one by one into his lap.

Vicky began screaming so loudly it was hard to believe that no one besides Victoria could hear her. "Someone do something! Quick! Take him in your arms, Victoria. Run your fingers through his hair like you always used to and tell him everything will be okay. Look way into his eyes and tell him we love him no matter what and we always will, forever and ever. Victoria, please! Do it! Do it now before it's too late!"

So in love, so sad, so confused was the princess that everything swirled around her in a hazy blur. She had such a big lump in her throat that she could not speak.

The king stood and began to pace back and forth, wringing his hands. "I resolve even the most difficult of problems—problems that affect the lives of the entire populace of this kingdom—yet I cannot think of a way to resolve this one for my own daughter and son-in-law."

"What God has joined together, let no man put asunder," the queen recited. "I am so very sorry, children, but this is one time I cannot advise you what to do."

The prince rose to return home. He hugged the king and queen good-bye harder and longer than he ever had before. He put his arm around the princess as she walked him to the palace entrance. Then he turned and whispered in her ear, "I love you, Princess. I always have and I always will—no matter what—forever."

Without waiting for the door to close behind him, the princess ran through the foyer, up the winding staircase, into her bedroom, and slammed the door shut. She threw herself across the soft pink quilts and cried, tried to decide what to do, and cried some more. Then, completely worn out, she fell into a troubled sleep.

Chapter Eight

To Do or Not to Do . . .

*T*HE princess awoke from her nap with a vivid image of a singing owl still fresh in her mind. The owl was wearing a straw hat, had a stethoscope dangling from his neck, and was playing tunes on a miniature banjo. She realized that she had been dreaming about none other than Henry Herbert Hoot, D.H.

She got up and wandered over to the window. There in the distance was the tree on the little hill where she had met Doc. Or thought she had met Doc. The tree seemed to be beckoning to her. She knew it was unlikely to find the owl there after so many years, even if he was real, but she felt irresistibly drawn to the tree just the same. Deciding she had enough time to get there before dark, she threw on a sweater and walked quickly down the staircase, passing the queen who was on her way up.

"I'm going for a walk, Mother," she said. "I'll be back soon."

Past the palace gardens she went and out to the little hill, shielding her eyes against the glare of the setting sun. The tree wasn't small anymore, but standing all alone against an orange sky, it looked even more lonely than she had remembered it.

Hopeful, she looked up into the branches. There wasn't an owl in sight. The sun dropped below the horizon, and her spirits dropped with it.

"Oh, Doc," she said aloud. "I really wish you were here. You're the only one I know who might be able to help me."

Disappointed, she sat for a while watching the darkening sky. A lone star appeared, shining brighter and brighter.

"Wish on the star, Victoria," Vicky suggested.

"Oh, Vicky. It's getting late. Anyway, it won't do any good. Doc isn't here."

"I bet he'll come if you wish on the star. Please, Victoria. Please."

"Okay, I'll try."

The princess looked up at the star.

> Star light, star bright,
> First star I see tonight,
> I wish I may, I wish I might
> Have the wish I wish tonight.

She closed her eyes tightly and wished her hardest for Doc to appear. Then she waited and waited, but nothing happened. She sank to the ground and covered her face with her hands.

A moment later banjo music began to play, and the voice she had wished to hear was singing:

> Heard you wishing on a star,
> So I flew here from afar.
> When you set your wishes free,
> Magically some come to be.

"Doc!" cried the princess, jumping to her feet and running over to the owl. "It's really you! I looked up in the tree, but I didn't see you."

"There's a lot you don't see, Princess."

"I see lots of things. I see you and your straw hat and your banjo. I see the tree and the sky and the star that I wished on."

"There are things to be seen that the eyes cannot behold," Doc said.

"What kind of things? Things like how wishing makes dreams come true?"

"If wishing makes dreams come true, why hasn't all your wishing gotten rid of the prince's evil spell?"

"How do you know about that?"

"A little bird told me. As a matter of fact, a whole flock of your feathered friends told me. They came in for a consultation when you stopped singing your songs. Their hearts were so heavy they could hardly fly."

"Yes, I know how that feels—I mean the heavy heart part." The princess sighed. "If only I could think of a way to get rid of the prince's evil spell, then I'd be happy and could sing with the birds again, and everything would be right with the world. You have to help me, Doc. I've tried everything. Nothing works."

"That's right, Princess. Nothing works."

"I thought for sure you'd know of *something*. Something I haven't thought of."

"I *do* know of something. It's *nothing*."

"Nothing?"

"Yes, nothing."

Victoria wrinkled her brow as she considered what Doc had said. "Do nothing?"

"Yes, Princess. Nothing is something you haven't tried yet. You must stop doing everything and start doing nothing. Do nothing and say nothing. No explaining, no defending, no setting things right, no pleading, no apologizing, no threatening, no worrying, no staying up nights thinking and planning and figuring out. Do you get the idea?"

"I can't simply do *nothing!*"

"By doing nothing you will actually be doing something—something that will help the prince by getting you out of his way."

"That's not a very nice thing to say!" the princess said indignantly. "How am I in his way? I'm only trying to help him."

"Forgive me, Princess. I didn't mean to offend you. But the prince is too busy looking at what's wrong with *you* to see what's wrong with *himself*. If you're doing nothing, he'll be more likely to see that he's doing something."

"I can't stop trying to help the prince. What would become of him?"

"What's become of him from your saying and doing everything that you have been? And what's become of you?"

"But he asked for my help."

"Just because someone asks for help is not reason enough to give it. Many times, helping ends up hurting."

The princess pressed her palms to her temples as her head began to pound. Vicky was getting more agitated by the minute.

"But we *have* to help the prince," Vicky blurted out. "If Victoria could only figure out what we're doing wrong, we could start doing it right, and then everything would be okay."

"Well, if it isn't little Vicky," Doc said. "Hello, there."

"How do you know about Vicky?" asked Victoria. "The birds couldn't have told you *that*."

"Owls know many things. They are very wise."

"She usually talks only to me, but sometimes she talks out loud so other people can hear her. Of course they think it's me. Sometimes I do, too. Well, she *is* me—I mean—she gets all mixed up with me, and then I can hardly tell who is who. Anyway, it's hard to explain."

"No need to, Princess," Doc replied. "Everyone has companions like Vicky. The *New Kingdom Journal of Medicine for Doctors of the Heart* has had numerous articles thoroughly explaining the phenomenon."

"Really? I thought I was the only one who—"

"We can discuss it some other time. But right now we must get back to the problem at hand. Both you and Vicky need to listen carefully."

"I will, but I don't think Vicky will," said Victoria. "She isn't very good at listening, especially when she's upset."

"We'll see. Come here and sit down," Doc said, calling the princess over with a wave of his wing. "What you've been doing wrong," he said, "is believing that you might have cast the evil spell on the prince and that if you could conjure up precisely the right magic elixir, you could make the spell go away."

"Yes, yes, that's it!" Vicky cried. "We need a magic 'lixir! But Victoria can't figure out what it is, even though she's very, very good at figuring stuff out."

"That's because the only one who can work magic *on* the prince *is* the prince," Doc said.

"Then it's completely hopeless. He can't do it," Victoria said. "He's tried."

"Yes, he *can*," Doc said. "But your happiness does not depend upon whether or not he *will*."

"Yes, it does," Vicky replied.

"It doesn't have to."

"What do we do?" Victoria asked.

"As I suggested before, do nothing. At least nothing that has to do with the prince and the spell. You can do something for yourself, however. As a matter of fact, there is much you can do for yourself."

The princess looked up pleadingly at Doc, her eyes swimming with tears. "I can't do another thing. I'm so sick and so tired. You're a doctor. Can't you help me?"

"Yes, of course," the owl replied, opening his black bag and taking out a prescription pad. He scrawled something across it with his folding quill pen, tore off the page, and handed it to the princess.

She squinted through her tears, trying to make out what he had written.

NAME: *Princess Victoria*
ADDRESS: *Royal Palace*

℞

TRUTH IS THE BEST MEDICINE
Take as much as you can, as
often as you can.

REFILLS: *Unlimited*
SIGNED: *Henry Herbert Hoot, D.H.*

"Truth is medicine?" the princess asked.

"Yes. The purest, most potent medicine in the universe. It's the only one that can help you."

"How can I find this truth?"

"You can begin with this," Doc said, reaching into his black bag again. He pulled out a small book with a lovely red rose on the cover and placed it in the princess's hand. She looked down at the gold script:

A Guide to Living Happily Ever After

For Princesses Who Are Sick and Tired
of Being Sick and Tired

Henry Herbert Hoot, D.H.

"That's all I ever wanted—to live happily ever after!" the princess said, clutching the book to her heart.

"Remember, reading the book is only the beginning," Doc said. "For *things* to change, *you* must change."

"Me?" Victoria said. "It's the *prince* who has to change."

"That is entirely up to the prince. You must try hard to keep that in mind."

"He could prob'ly change easier if he read the book," Vicky said tentatively. "Victoria could underline the important parts in red for him so—"

"As long as you keep *doing* what you've been doing, you'll keep *getting* what you've been getting," Doc said. "No more doing what doesn't work."

"But we know what's right for the prince better than anybody!" Vicky snapped.

"You must choose to be *happy* rather than *right*."

"Choose to be happy?" Victoria asked.

"Yes. Happiness is a choice."

"I can't even think about being happy right now," the princess said. "But I'd do anything for some peace and tranquillity."

"If that's true, Princess—really true—you are on your way to having it. But you must begin at the beginning. Go now and read the book."

"But, Doc—"

"Read the book," Doc said gently. "Then we'll talk some more."

"Are you sure you'll be here when I finish it?"

"As sure as one can be about anything, Princess. I took an oath to serve life."

"I'm so glad you came back into mine," Victoria said, giving the owl an affectionate hug.

With hope in her heart, the princess turned and headed back to her parents' palace, still clutching the book against her. She couldn't wait to get back to the quiet of her bedroom and begin reading.

As she walked across the foyer the king appeared, waving an envelope. "This just came for you by messenger."

The princess looked at her name on the front, written in the prince's usual style. Sadness overwhelmed her as she tore open the envelope and read the message inside:

> Roses are red,
> Violets are blue.
> Come home soon,
> We'll see this through.

She ran up to her bedroom and quickly gathered her things. She tossed them into her paisley overnight bag, putting the book in last, then hurried downstairs and told the king and queen she was going home and not to worry. For a moment she considered telling them that she was getting help from a specialist in matters of the heart, but thought better of it when she remembered how the queen had reacted the last time she tried to explain about Doc.

As her carriage pulled away from her parents' palace, the princess reached into her paisley bag and pulled out *A Guide to Living Happily Ever After*. Eagerly she opened it to the first page.

"When was the last time you looked into a mirror and were moved to dance?" it began. "The last time you sang a song that drew birds from the trees to gather and sing with you? The last time a vase of red roses filled you to the brim with happiness?"

The words began to blur as the princess's eyes glazed over with tears. *The last time . . . ?*

She couldn't remember.

Chapter Nine

A Guide to Living Happily Ever After

S O absorbed was the princess in *A Guide to Living Happily Ever After* that it seemed only moments later her carriage stopped in front of her palace. Hardly able to tear her eyes from the page, she stepped down from the carriage and walked to the palace entrance, the book still in hand, her finger holding her place.

The coachman placed her overnight bag on the entry floor inside the palace door. There was an unmistakable fragrance of roses in the air. She looked up at the hand-cut crystal vases that sat on white marble pedestals adorning each side of the entryway. Sure enough, the vases were filled with dozens of fresh red roses.

"Look! He picked roses for us, Victoria!" said Vicky. "He's getting better again."

"Maybe, Vicky. But he might have only picked the flowers because he's afraid we're going to leave him. You know he always gets nice when he thinks we may leave. It never lasts."

"Uh-uh. He still loves us. The roses prove it."

"I don't want to discuss this now, Vicky," said Victoria, eager to get back to the book.

Relieved that apparently the prince was not home, she ran upstairs to the master bedroom and flopped down on the big brass bed. The smell of roses made her glance over at the vase on her dressing table. It, too, had been filled with red roses.

Hoping Vicky wouldn't start up again, Victoria opened the book to where she had left off. She read and read, recognizing herself on every page—a fact that Vicky found terribly distressing. So much so that she kept interrupting Victoria's train of thought.

"That stuff's a bunch of baloney. You'd better throw out that book and forget all about Doc's dumb ideas. They're gonna make terrible trouble with the prince. I know it. I know it."

"What choice do we have?" Victoria answered. "We've already tried everything we could think of and none of it worked. Following Doc's advice is our only hope. He's very wise, Vicky. And he *is* a specialist."

♥ ♥

In the days that followed, the princess carried Doc's book around with her, reading a page here and a paragraph there at every opportunity. It was as if *A Guide to Living Happily Ever After* had been written just for her. Victoria underlined the important parts in red. So accustomed was she to doing this for the prince, that she had to keep reminding herself that this time she was doing it for herself. She went over and over the marked passages, especially when Mr. Hide was having one of his tirades.

"Words can hit as hard as a fist. You must try to keep out of the way," said Chapter Three, "Heated Arguments and Icy Silences." That was certainly true enough. Although they were not visible, the princess had the bruises to prove it.

Reading the book was no easy task. Sometimes the princess had to read the same sentence four or five times before the words made any sense to her. And some parts mysteriously kept drifting from her mind. She had to read them over and over again. Even then, often she couldn't remember them one minute after she turned the page. None of this had ever happened to her before, not even when she was studying long hours for final examinations while a student at Imperial University. But of course Vicky wasn't always trying to distract her, then.

Vicky vacillated between pouting and throwing tantrums in an effort to get Victoria to stop following Doc's advice.

"I don't believe the junk in that stupid book, and I'm not doing what it says!" Vicky yelled one day. "I don't care if it *does* say to stop playing games with the prince and doing our dance together. I *love* to play games and dance—you know that! I'm never gonna stop!"

"You don't understand, Vicky. It's not that kind of games and dancing. It's—"

"And all that mumbo-jumbo about how we can't fix the prince—like all the king's horses and all the king's men couldn't fix poor Humpty-Dumpty—and how he has to fix himself. And about how we're getting the king and queen and hurting and loving all mixed up, and all that stuff. It's getting me really, really mad!"

"Well, something's getting me really, really mad, too, Vicky—you! I'm knocking myself out trying to figure out what's really been going on here and why, and what to do about it, and it's hard enough without you fighting me all the way," Victoria said, looking back down into the book. But she had trouble concentrating after arguing with Vicky.

Doing *nothing* about the prince proved to be a lot more difficult than doing *something* had been. The princess took to keeping her hands buried deep in her skirt pockets to remind herself of her new hands-off policy. And she imagined her mouth taped shut at times she needed to remember to say nothing.

She often repeated Doc's words to herself: *For things*

to change, you must change. She threw all her effort into doing exactly that. After a while she was no longer spending every waking moment trying to help the prince get rid of the evil spell, nor trying to explain and to reason with him.

She tried even harder to stop worrying about what the prince would be like when he came home at the end of the day, planning what to say and do if he were to say this or do that, and being extra careful not to say or do or think or feel anything that would make him angry. But she found that *doing nothing* and *saying nothing*—as difficult as they were—were still much easier than *thinking nothing*. So in spite of her best efforts to stop them, the disturbing thoughts continued to race around and around relentlessly in her head.

Although her mind was painfully full, the rest of her was painfully empty. There was a great big void in her life—and in her—that nothing seemed able to fill. As time went on, each empty moment weighed more and more heavily on her hands . . . and her mind . . . and her heart.

She turned to *A Guide to Living Happily Ever After* for advice. It said that it was common for a person who was changing jobs to feel both full and empty. It suggested replacing the old job of focusing on the prince with new activities that focused on her.

The princess remembered how busy her hands and mind had been when she was testing recipes for her book, and she decided to try cooking again. She went through the motions from morning until night, but except for some brief respites the flurry of thoughts persisted, and she felt as empty as ever.

She thought that being among the roses might make her feel better, so she tried working in the garden from sunup to sundown. But that only depressed her more. The roses kept reminding her of the prince.

She stayed in bed for days at a time, taking the relaxer remedy the palace chief physician had given her, but that didn't work either.

The princess decided she had to try something new. She thought and thought until she came up with a list of things to do that might work better than those she had already tried. The most promising idea on the list was shopping. She had heard that it did wonders for one's spirit and was especially good for filling empty hours and emptying overfilled minds.

The next morning the princess was waiting by the door of the Old Kingdom General Store when it opened. She headed for the cloth department and chose several bolts from which she had pieces cut. She planned to take them to the royal dressmaker, but she got so involved in her shopping that she never got there.

By the time the store closed, she had bags and bags of hats, with flowers and without, and gloves—satin, leather, and wool—each in several colors. There were baubles of every size and shape, and shoes with matching pocketbooks. There were so many bags that it took three clerks and her coachman to load them into her carriage.

After that, she shopped every day from opening until closing and took home so many things that her wardrobe closets were stuffed full. Two of them wouldn't even shut. She finally converted one of the guest rooms into a closet and very nearly filled that up, too.

"Are you going on a trip, Victoria?" the queen asked when she stopped by for a brief visit one day. "You have more clothing here than the Old Kingdom General Store! How on earth will you ever wear it all?"

But knowing she would never wear it all didn't deter the princess from going back and buying more, as the empty place within her was a big as ever. Day after day she shopped until she dropped. One night she was accidentally locked in the store when it closed—and she didn't much care. It was then that she realized how barren and meaningless her life had become and how hopeless and helpless *she* had become.

The next day she desperately flipped through the pages of *A Guide to Living Happily Ever After* searching for something that would tell her what to do. She soon came upon, "*Cast out* your painful thoughts and feelings by *writing* them out."

The princess got her quill pen and a piece of parchment. Then she sat down at her dressing table to write, but her mind went blank, and her pain was stuffed so far down inside her that it got stuck and couldn't come out. She reached over and pulled her little music box closer, remembering the many hours she had spent listening to it and dreaming. She turned the key. The elegant couple on top began their dance to the melody of "Someday My Prince Will Come."

As she listened to the tinkling notes of her favorite song, the pain deep inside her began to rise higher and higher. The princess grabbed her pen, and as her agony broke loose and burst forth she poured it out onto the parchment, then onto another and another—moaning all the while and dripping so many tears that the ink formed little rivulets that ran off the edges of the pages.

Every day after that, the princess read and reread and thought and rethought various sections of *A Guide to Living Happily Ever After*. Often, she discovered, she could open the book to any page and find that the exact information she needed most at that moment was right there, as if it had stepped forward, volunteering to come to her aid.

"Happiness is a choice," one such message said. She turned the phrase over and over in her mind, recalling that Doc had told her the same thing, but happiness had seemed so distant, so unreachable. . . .

She continued reading: "Once the choice has been made, you should practice being happy as best you can, even if you have to fake it till you make it." Then there was an explanation of how thoughts follow actions and feelings follow thoughts.

The princess carefully considered what she had read. Suddenly she had an idea. She tore up her old list of things to do and made a new one. The first thing on it was to resume the royal responsibilities she had abandoned when all her time was being taken up with helping the prince. She volunteered to direct the annual children's play at the Sovereignty Orphanage and signed up for a floral design class at Imperial University. Most of the time she had to force herself to go, but she went, regardless, making good use of her ability to smile on the outside while crying on the inside and repeating to herself, "Fake it till you make it. Fake it till you make it. Fake it till you make it."

Soon the princess began to prepare some of her favorite recipes again, and she tried her hardest to enjoy eating them, even though Mr. Hide usually showed up for supper determined to make things unpleasant.

Gradually she spent less time walking on eggs and waiting for the other shoe to drop. And she spent more time thinking about things other than herself and how bad she felt.

One afternoon as she gathered ingredients for her Broccoli Fettuccine with Pistachio Pesto Sauce, she noticed a pleasant sound she hadn't heard in a very long time—the sound of her own voice, humming.

Later, as she busily chopped pistachio nuts, she lapsed into song, much to her surprise. Suddenly a plump bluebird flew in through one of the kitchen windows and misjudging its landing, plopped down right in the middle of the mound of chopped nuts.

"Not *you* again!" she said with a giggle, lifting up the

squirming bird and brushing pistachio crumbs from its feet as she had the time before. "Those pistachios sure do get in your way, don't they, my funny little friend?" She peered into the bluebird's face. "Did you come to sing with me?" she asked. "Okay, then. Let's sing."

She began her song again, and soon her other feathered friends joined them. The kitchen came alive with their melodious chirping. As the sweet sound of their harmony floated throughout the room, she realized how much she had been missing.

After that, the princess took even better care of herself. But the better care she took and the less she allowed the prince to pull her into his tirades, the angrier he grew.

"You don't love me anymore," he yelled one day from the sitting room doorway as she clipped recipes from the food section of the *Kingdom Times*.

She reminded herself to remain calm. She knew better than to get drawn into a verbal sparring match that would leave her feeling for days afterward as if she had been run over by a carriage.

"Oh, I'm sorry you feel that way," she replied in the noncommittal tone suggested by *A Guide to Living Happily Ever After*.

"Oh, oh," he mimicked, walking over and standing in front of her. "Is that all you have to say? You used to say plenty!"

"I don't want to fight with you," she risked replying.

"Why not, Miss Perfect? Afraid you'll lose?"

How could it all have come to this? Although she knew better, she couldn't help asking one more time, "When did I become the enemy?"

"I don't know. Maybe it was the day you started helping me."

"But you asked for my help. Pleaded for—"

"No, I didn't! I never asked for your help. And I never wanted it."

The usual, unsettling confusion overtook her.

"You call what you were doing, helping me? Helping me to do what? To change, because what I am isn't good enough for you?"

"That's not fair," the shaken princess heard herself say. "I love you. I miss you. I want you back. I want *us* back. I have no idea what's going on. What do I have to do to get through to you?"

"You don't love me. You probably never did. The prince you wanted is the one you dreamed of, not the one you have."

"But I *did* have him. *You* were him. You were everything I wanted my prince to be, until the evil spell came over you."

"You just don't listen! I've told you before, that prince is dead. But you refuse to believe it."

"I can't help it. I know he's still in there. Every so often, I see him. I feel him."

"You always have had trouble believing the truth, even when you can see it with your own eyes. Look at me," he said, taking her chin roughly in his hand and pulling it toward him. "Look hard," he demanded. "What you see is what you get. And you obviously don't want it. You don't *love* me. You can't *stand* me. Well, I've got news for you. I can't stand you either, so what do you think of that, Miss Icky Picky Princess, Miss Royal Pain—"

"Stop it! Stop it!" Vicky screamed.

Victoria's mind was reeling. . . . Doc. She had to see Doc.

The princess grabbed the arm of the sofa to steady herself as she stood up. In a daze, she walked toward the sitting room door, but the prince got there first and blocked her way. "Where do you think you're going?" he thundered.

Her heart was pounding. "I-I don't know—just somewhere else— I mean—"

"I'm not through with you yet."

"I've heard enough. I-I can't stand any more."

"*I'll* decide when you've heard enough," he said, grabbing her by the arm.

"Let go, you're hurting me— Let go!"

He clenched his teeth, glared at her, and squeezed tighter.

"Please, let go," she cried, trying to pull away from his iron grip.

Suddenly he released her arm, sending her flying to the floor. "You want to go? Go!"

The princess struggled with her tangled skirts as she tried to stand up. Then, once on her feet, she bolted from the room and rushed down the long hall toward the front doors of the palace, the prince shouting after her.

"You and your *big* dreams. You don't *deserve* to live happily ever after! Do you hear me? You don't deserve it!"

PART III

Chapter Ten

The Path of Truth

S Victoria called for her carriage, Vicky's voice exploded in her head. "I don't wanna go see Doc. I told you that quacky doctor and his stupid book would ruin everything. The prince hates us! He hates us! And it's all your fault!"

Victoria didn't have the energy to argue. As the carriage pulled away, she buried her head in her hands, trying not to listen to Vicky's carrying on. Hopefully, Doc would know what to do.

The princess went as far as she could in the carriage, instructed the coachman to wait, then continued on foot until she reached the tree on the hill, all the while trying to ignore the incessant muttering in her head.

"Doc—Doc—where are you? Please, I need you," she wailed, looking all around. Not seeing the owl anywhere, she began to tremble. What if she couldn't find him? What would she do?

"Doc, I need you right now. This minute, please!"

"Impatience, dear Princess, is nothing more than ignorance of what is supposed to be happening in the present moment," Doc said, appearing out of nowhere.

"Oh, Doc. There you are. Thank heavens! I don't know what to do. Nothing is working. Or rather, nothing isn't working—I mean— Oh, Doc, I've tried so hard for so long to— What's the use? I give up."

"It is better to give *in* than to give *up*."

"What do you mean?" she asked.

"One gives up out of hopelessness, but one gives in out of acceptance."

"Acceptance?"

"Yes. Acceptance of the things one cannot change."

Victoria pondered this for a moment. "You mean I have no choice but to accept the prince and all the despicable things he says and does that keep me shaking and churning and crying all the time?"

"One always has choices," Doc replied. "But changing someone else is not one of them."

"I know that now, but what other choices do I have?" the princess asked.

"You can choose not to react to the things he says and does. To carry on your life as best you can and live as happily as you can, accepting that he will probably continue saying and doing whatever he has been saying and doing."

"That's what I've been trying to do ever since you told me about doing nothing and gave me *A Guide to Living Happily Ever After*. But I can't always do it, even though I keep my hands in my skirt pockets to remind me of my new hands-off policy with the prince and imagine that I have tape over my mouth so I remember to say nothing. There's this gigantic black cloud hanging over me all the time—even when I'm fulfilling my royal responsibilities or directing the children's play at the orphanage or arranging flowers in class at the university or making one of my favorite recipes." The princess sighed. "So what other choices do I have?"

"You can choose not to be where the prince is."

"Are you saying that I should leave him?"

"I'm not suggesting anything, but it *is* one of your choices."

Vicky couldn't keep quiet one more second. Her voice

boomed in Victoria's head. "I'm never leaving the prince or giving up on him, or giving in, or whatever you call it! Never. Do you hear me! Never, ever!"

"Vicky, please! I can't take this anymore," Victoria cried, throwing her hands up in the air. "I wish I could run away."

"There is no more hope of running from one's problems than there is of running from one's shadow. It never works to run away *from*. Only to move *toward*," Doc said.

"Everything is such a mess. Nothing is the way I thought it was. My whole life is falling apart, and I don't have the strength to stop it." The princess lowered her head and grew silent.

"You've shown great strength getting through all that you have."

"I don't feel very strong. I'm all worn out, and I'm still shaking and churning and—"

"And you'll keep right on being worn out and shaking and churning until you decide whether to stay or leave, and make peace with whichever you choose."

Victoria contemplated his words. "Whenever I have a big decision to make, I always—"

"Yes, I know," Doc said, handing her his folding quill pen and a piece of parchment from his bag.

On the top left side of the parchment, she wrote: "Pros—For Staying." On the right side she wrote: "Cons—Against Staying." She looked off thoughtfully into the distance for a moment. Then the quill began to fly across the page.

"Put down that he works very hard at the embassy," Vicky urged, "and that he comes straight home to us every night and that he's very handsome and smart and fun and good at fixing stuff. And put down that he always brought us chicken soup when we were sick and told us we're the fairest of them all and picked beautiful roses for us. Oh, and be sure to put down that he—"

"Vicky, please! I can't think with you jabbering at me."

"Then stop 'xaggerating the bad stuff about him. I bet lots of princes are much, much worse than him. He's not *that* bad. I can stand it if you can."

"It's true. He does have a lot of good qualities," Victoria said, her quill moving to the list of reasons for staying. But soon the list against staying began to grow again. The longer it grew, the more panicky Vicky became.

"You're making a big mistake, Victoria. How do you know it'll be any better with some other prince? We could look our whole lives long and never find another prince to love us. We'll be all alone forever, and it'll be all *your* fault!" Vicky wailed.

A few minutes later Victoria looked up from her list, tears running down her cheeks. "But I still love him, Doc," she said, "even though the Con list is much longer than the Pro list. And I know he loves me, at least the real prince does—the Dr. Chuckle part, way inside. How can I possibly leave?"

"Love feels good," Doc said. "If it doesn't feel good, it isn't love."

"But it *feels* like love."

"If you're in pain more often than you are happy, it isn't love. It's something else. Something that keeps you trapped in a prison of sorts, unable to see that the door to freedom is standing wide open before you."

The more the princess thought of leaving the prince, the mightier became the grip that pulled her back to him. But she knew that whatever the feeling was—love or not—if she let it win out, she would indeed be returning to a prison, a prison of pain that had become unbearable. She sat biting her lip and fighting to keep from being consumed by the overwhelming feeling that she was about to shrivel up and die on the spot.

Finally she turned to Doc, who sat silently awaiting her decision. Her voice quivering, she said, "I know I must leave, but where will I go?"

"You will continue on the Path of Truth."

"You mean I've already been on it?"

"Yes. Ever since the day I gave you the prescription and you filled it by beginning to read the book."

"Why didn't I notice the path?"

"It was there, but often one does not see the path until one has traveled on it for some distance. One does not see what one is not ready to see."

"Well, I've learned some things about truth already," the princess said quietly. "The truth is that fairy tales don't come true and living happily ever after is nothing more than a childish dream."

"On the contrary, Princess, fairy tales *do* come true," Doc said. "But they are often different than one first envisions them. Your happy ending awaits you on the path."

"Really?" she said, her face brightening. "A *different* fairy tale?" The princess had never considered the possibility that she could live happily ever after without being rescued by a courageous, charming, handsome prince charging up on a big white stallion, scooping her up, and carrying her off into the sunset. She sighed. "But I've thought happiness awaited me before, and look where it got me."

"It got you to where you are now."

"What's so good about where I am now?" Victoria asked.

"You'll find the answer to that on the path."

She hesitated. "I don't want to go by myself. Can you show me the way?"

"I would if I could, Princess," Doc replied gently. "But one must find one's own way."

"I'm afraid I might get lost," she said.

"You wouldn't be the first who did. But have no fear. Your heart knows the way."

"My heart wants me to go home. I'm not sure it makes sense to do this."

"Truth makes sense of everything."

"You are so wise, Doc. You must already know all about truth. Why don't you tell me so I won't have to go looking for it?"

"One can never learn truth from another. One must discover it for oneself."

"All right then," she said sorrowfully. "I guess I'll go home and pack a few things."

"You already have all that you need. You simply aren't aware of it. But do as you wish. I'll wait here to give you some last-minute instructions."

"I'm not going anywhere!" Vicky yelled. "We don't have to leave the prince. I'll convince him that we love him and we need him, and he'll take us in his arms and tell us he's so very sorry, that it's all been a big mistake. His eyes'll sparkle brighter than ever before, and we'll know they sparkle for us. He'll pick beautiful red roses from our garden, and we'll put them all around the palace in the vases. All will be right with the world again. I promise it'll work this time, Victoria. Cross my heart and hope to die, kiss a—"

"Oh, Vicky, my poor, sweet little Vicky. It's over," Victoria replied faintly.

"No, no. It's not. It can't be! It'll never be over. *Never!* Do you hear me!" Vicky screamed hysterically. "I'd *die* without him."

"No, Vicky. You'd die *with* him—and so would I."

Her mind made up, Victoria walked briskly to her

waiting carriage and returned to the palace. She went up the staircase and into the master bedroom. She threw a few necessities into her paisley overnight bag, then stuck in a copy of the *Royal Family Natural Gourmet Recipe Book.* Having come to rely upon *A Guide to Living Happily Ever After,* she tossed that in, too.

She rolled up her treasured little glass slippers etched with her initials in one of her soft wool scarves and secured it with a hair ribbon, then carefully placed them in the bag. She thought about not taking her music box because the overnight bag was getting heavy—and lately the music made her too sad anyway—but somehow she couldn't leave it behind.

Then thinking that the Royal Family Map might come in handy on her journey, the princess threw open the white wooden hope chest with clusters of hand-carved roses at the corners and reached inside. She riffled through until her fingers felt the ragged edges of the old, rolled parchment. She tossed the map into the overnight bag. Almost as an afterthought, she threw in Doc's prescription and fastened the bag, reminding herself to stop at the kitchen before leaving to get some food to take along. All the while Vicky's screaming was giving Victoria a monstrous headache.

The princess inched over to the big brass bed, feeling compelled to run her hand over the satin bedcovering that had time and time again been drenched by her tears. But all she remembered were the times the prince had held her in his arms and whispered words of love. She took a deep breath, savoring the aroma of the prince's favorite cologne, which still lingered in the air. So filled with her own tears was she that she feared if she let them out all at once, she would surely drown.

Doubt came suddenly like a flash of lightning and lasted about as long.

"I must do this. I must," Victoria reminded herself, her voice sounding as if it belonged to someone else. Nothing felt real. She half expected someone to wake her from the nightmare.

She went to her dressing table, opened the center drawer, and looked at the small stack of white parchment thank-you notepapers left over from her wedding. She removed a note from the drawer, opened it, and on the inside wrote:

> Roses are red,
> Violets are blue.
> Sad as it is,
> I must leave you.

She leaned the note against the vase of roses and started toward the door, then stopped to take a last look around the bedroom she had shared for years with her prince. Her eyes locked on the note and vase of red roses. She had been so preoccupied, she hadn't even noticed how wilted the flowers were, and that shriveled petals had fallen from their stems and lay in little piles around the bottom of the vase.

She set down the overnight bag and went over to the dressing table. Her throat was taut, her hands trembling.

"No!" Vicky shouted. "Don't!"

"We picked them over a week ago, Vicky," Victoria replied. "They must have been dropping petals for days."

"No, don't throw them away! They may come back!"

They may come back? . . . They may come back? Could they possibly? she wondered.

Victoria sighed. "No, Vicky. They aren't ever coming back," she said gently. "And neither are we."

♥ ♥

Several times during the carriage ride back to the tree where Doc awaited her, the princess had the coachman turn the carriage around and head back home. Each time, only moments later, she instructed him to turn around and continue toward the tree again.

It was no wonder that Victoria's conviction to leave kept slipping, as Vicky was frightening her, ranting and raving about how lost and scared they would be without the prince and how no one would ever want them or love them again and how they would while away the years, sad and lonely, and finally die all alone.

The princess stepped from the carriage, reached for her paisley overnight bag, and sent the coachman on his way, trembling as she watched him drive off. She walked slowly toward the little hill, aware that each step she took was a step away from the prince she loved and all she had ever known.

As she approached the tree, the princess saw Doc, straw hat on his head, perched on a lower branch, playing his banjo. She heard his mellow voice singing:

> I have no palace, have no horse,
> Yet I'm flying right on course.
> I've trees of green and skies of blue,
> Say, that might be a start for you.

"*Some* start this is. I feel like I'm finished," the princess said, looking up at him sadly. "It's hard to believe there's anything to look forward to."

"Oh, but there *is*, Princess," responded Doc. "Though undoubtedly difficult for you to believe right now, you have much to look forward to—for the greater the pain, the greater the opportunity."

"Opportunity? For what?"

"In this case, for a wonderful new life. Today is the

beginning of yours."

"It sure doesn't feel like it," the princess said. "I don't want to do this. I do so wish I didn't have to. But I know I must."

"The ability to do what is *best* when it is different from what one *wants,* is a sign of maturity," Doc said, dropping lightly to the ground. "Of course, that doesn't make it any less difficult."

"I think I had better get started before I change my mind again. But how can I go on a path that I can't even see?"

"Look again, Princess," Doc suggested.

The princess gasped. "Where did that come from?" she asked, pointing to a path that suddenly appeared right in front of her, its rocky surface twisting and turning out to a steep rise that stretched far into the distance. "Why didn't I ever see it before?"

"Were you ever truly willing to look before?"

"No, I guess I wasn't," she replied, looking out at the path. "I can't see where it ends."

"It doesn't."

"It doesn't end? But how will I know I'm going in the right direction if I can't keep my eye on where I'm supposed to end up?"

"There are signposts. Unfortunately, people don't always read them. Sometimes they are difficult to see. You must watch carefully for them."

"It looks very difficult," the princess said. "I could get hurt. Or lost. Or both."

"You have already been both, and you survived. This, too, you shall survive."

"I don't think I'm strong enough to go through all that. I'll get too weak to go on," she said, growing more frightened with each passing moment.

"On the contrary," Doc replied. "The more you go

through, the more opportunity you'll have to grow strong. Remember what I said about pain and opportunity."

"I'm not so sure about this. I had no idea what I was getting into when I said I would go."

"No one ever said that getting to the truth would be easy. You will need to be many things—an explorer, navigator, trailblazer, and more—for the path winds through some rugged terrain. It is known to have many obstacles. Potholes that lie in wait for unaware travelers. Blankets of pebbles that wobble and roll beneath one's feet. And boulders—some that seem the size of mountains and as immovable—that block the way. For many things get in the way of truth, some big, others small."

"It sounds like the perfect place to be rescued." Then she remembered. "I don't suppose my prince will come and rescue me just in the nick of time?"

Doc smiled. "See, you're learning already. Now I must give you some important last-minute instructions. Are you ready?"

"I guess so."

"You must follow the path no matter what and seek the truth that awaits you there. Let nothing deter you from your search for the truth that will heal you."

"How will I know truth when I find it?"

"Truth becomes clearer and clearer as one travels the path. Follow it faithfully, and eventually you'll come upon the Temple of Truth, House of the Sacred Scroll."

"The Temple of Truth? I've never heard of it. What is it like? And what's the Sacred Scroll?"

"The temple is one of the most beautiful places in the universe, in more ways than one can imagine. Once you pass through its portals, you will be changed forever. The Sacred Scroll will awaken your mind and set your heart free. You will find peace and serenity and learn the secret of true love—the kind you've dreamed of all your life. You will be well on your way to making your fairy tale come true."

"Oh, Doc. That's what I want more than anything in the world!"

The owl fanned out his wings high in the air. "Then you shall have it. Go forth, dear Princess, and plant the seeds of truth from which will grow peace, love, and happiness."

"I hope I can figure out how," she said. "The only thing I ever planted was roses."

She picked up her paisley overnight bag. Then watching for potholes, pebbles, boulders, and such, she took one fearful step after another along the Path of Truth, shaking her head and mumbling to herself, "I can't believe I'm really doing this."

Chapter Eleven

The Sea of Emotion

*T*HE princess walked cautiously along the winding dirt path, her paisley overnight bag growing heavier by the minute. Her mind was completely preoccupied with figuring out what had gone wrong with the prince, exactly when it began, what could have caused it, who was to blame, and what she might have said or done differently that might have changed things. She replayed her memories in every detail, searching for answers, until her head throbbed, but she still couldn't stop trying to figure it all out.

Finally she collapsed by an old, jagged tree stump surrounded by shrubbery that looked as if it desperately needed water. She was afraid that soon she would, too, as she thought of her meager supply running out.

"Maybe we'll die of thirst before we twist our ankle in a pothole or slip on some pebbles or run smack dab into a big boulder," said Vicky, who had been babbling unintelligibly ever since they had set out on the path.

"Oh, Vicky, for heaven's sake! The last thing I need now is for you to start up with me."

"Well, the last thing *I* need is for us to be all alone on this awful, dusty path full of half-dead bushes, not knowing where we're going."

Victoria reached into the overnight bag and rummaged around until she found the Royal Family Map. She pulled off the silver band and carefully unrolled the brittle parchment.

"Maybe this will help us find our way," she said, looking intently at the map as she took a bite from one of the biscuits she had brought with her.

"The only *way* I wanna find is our way home," Vicky blurted out. "And we'd better get there fast before the prince finds a new princess to love."

"There's nothing I can do about that," Victoria said, her heart pounding rapidly at the thought.

"But you have to, or he'll pick handfuls of beautiful red roses for her and put them in crystal vases all around the palace, and his strong arms will hold her close and—"

"He wouldn't be that way with us even if we did go home. You know he wouldn't."

"Why can't everything be the way it was before?" Vicky lamented.

"It can't, that's all."

"But her fingers will stroke his jet black hair—*our* prince's jet black hair—and his face'll light up when she walks into the room, and his eyes will sparkle—*our* sparkle—just for her." Vicky moaned. "I can't stand it, I can't stand it! Please, please, we have to go home right now!"

Victoria covered her ears with her hands, struggling not to hear Vicky's words. But she did hear them, loud and clear. And they conjured up a vivid mental picture of another princess holding and loving *her* prince. Her wonderful, charming, handsome, very own prince.

"I don't know what to do, Vicky. I can't even figure out what went wrong or whose fault it was. But I do know we can't go home. You know we can't, don't you?"

"But I can't live without him. I can't!" Vicky screamed. "It feels like someone chopped off our arms and legs."

"That's a horrible thing to say!" Victoria replied, then added softly, "Horrible, but true. Doc never told us it would be like this."

At that moment a mass of heavy-looking, dark clouds rolled in front of the sun, and Victoria's world grew dim with doubt. She shuddered as a cool breeze began to blow. She wasn't prepared for a storm.

"We had better look for shelter," Victoria said, hurriedly stuffing the map back into the overnight bag as droplets of rain began to fall.

"Look," Vicky said, starting to cry. "The whole world's as sad as we are."

That made Victoria begin to cry, too. The harder it rained, the harder they cried. The harder they cried, the harder it rained. It seemed as if the whole world was crying with them.

There was so much rain and so many tears that puddles formed—first small ones, then large ones. The rain and tears continued to pour, turning the puddles into a steady stream of churning water that traveled faster and faster, until it swelled into a flood that gushed with such force that it swept along with it everything that wasn't firmly grounded.

The princess was so distraught that she didn't notice what was happening until a torrent of rushing water snatched her up and swept her down the path, bumping and scraping and bouncing and twisting her along.

"I'm afraid of the water!" Vicky yelled.

"I know," Victoria shouted back. "That's why we couldn't take swimming lessons."

"You should've made me!"

"This is no time to talk about it!" Victoria hollered, grabbing desperately at the branches of rooted bushes as they flew past. But in spite of her best efforts, the princess was washed uncontrollably down the path.

"Victoria. Look!" But it was already too late. A gigantic sea of water loomed before them. "Yipes! We're going off the deep end!"

The princess was hurled, breathless and terrified, into the Sea of Emotion. Sharp rocks and pieces of broken branches swirled in the icy water around her as she struggled wildly to stay afloat. A strong undercurrent tugged at her feet, while pellets of rain relentlessly pounded at her face and head.

"We're gonna drown for sure!" cried Vicky between mouthfuls of salty water. "I wish the prince was here to help us."

The princess kept splashing and kicking, calling out for someone to save her. As she was being sucked down again into the sea, she caught a glimpse of something in the distance. If only she could get to it.

When she surfaced, it was still there. It appeared to be a ship, rolling and pitching toward her. "Help! Save me!" she called as loudly as she could, hoping that whoever was on the ship had had some experience in rescuing people. Perhaps it was a courageous, charming, handsome prince unexpectedly caught in the storm while out for a cruise. Or maybe it was one of the kingdom's Royal Navy ships.

She kept calling out, but no one answered. As the vessel came closer, she saw why. There was no one in it. And it was much smaller than she had first thought—it was a rowboat.

When the craft reached her, she grabbed the side and tried as hard as she could to pull herself up into the safety of the hull, but she was too weak. If only she could rest for a minute, she thought, perhaps she could muster up the strength. So she held on tight, first with one hand, then the other. Finally, with one strong pull, she toppled over the side and fell in. Exhausted, she stayed right where she landed, sprawled out on the bottom of the rickety boat on top of two old wooden oars.

"Whew! I thought we were gonna drown for sure," said Vicky. "What're we gonna do now?"

"As soon as I've got the energy, we're going to use these oars to get ourselves back to land. All I have to do is figure out which way that is."

The princess pulled herself up with great effort and looked to the north—or was it the south? she wondered. Or—well, it didn't really seem to matter as long as she spotted land. But for as far as she could see in every direction, there was nothing but the dark, turbulent sea.

"It's awful scary out there," Vicky said in a trembling voice.

"Don't be afraid. Everything will be all right once I figure out which way to go."

"Your figuring out stuff's what got us into this mess in the first place. I wanna go home!"

"If you don't quiet down and let me think, we may die here."

"I *told* you we'd die if we left the prince," Vicky said accusingly. "You didn't believe me. You should've believed me, Victoria."

"Vicky, please! I don't have time for this now."

"It isn't fair! Of all the princes in the kingdom, why did *ours* have to be the one to get the evil spell?"

"I can only figure out one thing at a time, Vicky."

"He promised to love us and cherish us forever and ever. I should've made him say, 'Cross my heart and hope to die, kiss a lizard in one try'—'cause he broke his promise! He's mean. He's meaner than mean. It's all his fault we had to leave. I hate him! He ruined everything. Our whole life. I can't stand it. I can't stand it!" Vicky shouted, throwing herself onto the bottom of the boat and kicking her feet and pounding her fists until they were bruised and throbbing. "It's all wrong. Everything's all wrong. It's not fair! And now we're gonna die!"

"Stop it! Stop it! Do you hear me?" Victoria yelled. "You have to calm down. I can't think with you screaming and beating on the boat."

The sky grew darker yet. A moment later the heavens seemed to split wide open. Gigantic raindrops pelted the sea. The small boat tossed violently as the sea unleashed its fury. The princess clung to the side, but the storm's rage was no match for her or the little boat. She was thrown unmercifully from one side of the boat to the other. Twice she almost fell overboard.

"I wanna go home!" Vicky called into the howling wind. "Somebody help us, please, please! Doc! Somebody! Anybody! Get us out of the storm and off this boat and make the prince nice like he used to be and get us home, and I'll be better than I've ever been before, in every way. I-I'll be perfect. I'll do anything—whatever you want. I promise, really, truly promise. I'd cross my heart and hope to die, but as you can prob'ly see, my arms are busy. And anyway this doesn't seem like the best time to hope to die!"

The bottom of the boat began to fill with water. The princess frantically scooped up handfuls and dumped them over the side. But the water slowly continued to rise.

"Some lifeboat this turned out to be," Victoria said.

"It's all my fault," Vicky hollered. "I know it. I prob'ly punched a hole in the bottom of the boat with my fist when I got so mad before."

"I doubt it, Vicky. This boat's just old and too small for all this rain and the splashing waves." Victoria snatched the oars from the rising water. "We're getting out of here right now."

"But we don't know which way to go."

"Anywhere is better than here," Victoria replied, beginning to row madly. But the current kept pushing the boat back.

"Hurry up! We have to get off this boat before it sinks."

"I'm trying!" Victoria shouted.

As night fell the princess was still methodically pushing and pulling the oars as hard as she could, her arms aching. The boat was half filled with water. Vicky grew panicky.

"What if we're going the wrong way or if there isn't any land no matter which way we go or if we're going in circles and we can't even tell or if . . ."

Silently, Victoria continued to row. By morning, her arms had grown so weak that she could row no longer. She let go of the oars. "I'm afraid we're going to go down with the boat."

"It doesn't matter," Vicky said. "What've we got to live for, anyway? Even our paisley bag is gone."

As the boat rode lower and lower in the water, Victoria kept trying to come up with a new plan. If only she had something to use for signaling another boat.

"It looks like you're nearly up to your neck in trouble," a voice called to her.

"Yes, and the way things are going, I'll soon be in over my head," Victoria replied without hesitation.

"Hmm. Very clever," the voice said. "Also very true, I'm afraid, unless you do something to save yourself."

"Save myself? That's what I've been trying to— Hey, who are you? Where are you?" the princess asked, looking all around. "Help! Please help me!"

Suddenly a shiny gray head appeared on the surface of the water. "Hello, there," it said, fluttering long eyelashes that reminded the princess of the prince. "I'm Dolly. Dolly the Dolphin. And I would ask, How do you do? But I can clearly see that you aren't doing at all well at the moment. At least you have both oars in the water, which is considerably more than I can say of some others I have found here."

"A dolphin! A talking dolphin! I know dolphins talk to one another, but I had no idea— And now you've come to rescue me. And just in the nick of time! Funny, somehow I always thought I'd be rescued by a prince."

"No one can rescue you, my dear. Not me, not a prince, not anyone. An often elusive fact, even for one who is good at figuring out things."

"You mean you're going to let me drown?" she asked in amazement.

"No, I mean *you're* going to let you drown—either now or the next time—unless you learn to swim, that is."

"The next time? What do you mean, 'the next time'?"

"Even if I were to carry you on my back from this storm and deliver you safely to solid ground, it would only be a matter of time until the next storm hits and you would inevitably find yourself in jeopardy again, for there are many storms to weather on the path."

"I'm still trying to figure out a way not to drown in *this* one," Victoria said.

"As I told you, the way to avoid drowning is to learn to swim."

"But Vicky has always refused."

"Then you'll spend your whole life trying to keep from drowning—as you are now—watching and waiting for the one perfect lifeboat to save you once and for all."

"Yes! Yes! That's 'xactly what we need!" Vicky blurted out. "Do you think you could find us one real fast?"

"Even if I could, it probably wouldn't do you much good. It's common for one's lifeboats to sink," Dolly said.

"Lifeboats aren't s'posed to sink," Vicky replied indignantly. "They're s'posed to save people!"

"Many things don't do what we think they're supposed to do. Lifeboats, for example, frequently drown the very people they are supposedly saving."

"Really?" Victoria asked.

"Yes. When you first spotted your boat, didn't you think it was going to save you? And didn't it turn out to be small and old and so rickety that it filled with water?"

"I guess so," Vicky mumbled.

"And aren't you desperately holding on, even though it's going down and threatens to take you down with it?"

"I s'pose," Vicky said sulkily. Then suddenly she brightened. "I know! You could give us a ride out of here. You'd make it through the storm. You're a dolphin, and dolphins are really good swimmers. And they're smart, too. I bet you know 'xactly where the land is."

"I *could* do it, but I *won't*."

"Why not?"

"Because when you give a man a fish, you feed him today. When you teach him how to fish, you feed him for life. That's why."

"Who cares about some stupid man and his fish!" Vicky said, growing frustrated. "You have to help us get out of here before the water comes up any higher."

"I can only help by teaching you how to help yourselves."

"Help ourselves? How can we do that?" Victoria asked.

"By jumping ship, so to speak," the dolphin answered.

"What's that mean, Victoria?"

"It means get off the boat."

"You don't understand!" Vicky shouted at the dolphin. "We already told you, we can't swim!"

"It is *you* who doesn't understand. You *can* swim. You've simply chosen not to. I can teach you how."

"We're freezing and tired, and anyway, the water's too rough," Vicky said with finality. "We'd prob'ly drown if we tried to learn now."

"You'll *surely* drown if you *don't* try to learn now."

Vicky began screaming and clutching on to the side of

the boat. "No, no. I don't wanna leave the boat!"

"One can feel as if one is drowning and still survive. It is important to remember that," Dolly said.

"We're not gonna be around to 'member anything," Vicky yelled.

"Some people have to hit bottom before they are willing to learn how to save themselves. And even then, some still won't risk trying. You came on this journey to avoid going down with *one* sinking ship," Dolly said. "Are you sure you want to let yourself go down with this one?"

"I don't get it," Vicky replied. "We weren't even *on* another ship."

"Dolly means the prince," Victoria said. "He was the other ship, in a way. That was the first time we had to decide whether to stay and sink, or leave and try to swim. If we had stayed with him, we soon would have drowned in our own tears. And if we stay here in the boat, we'll drown in the sea. Do you understand?"

Dolly flipped her fin. "Yes, sometimes you need to stop *holding* on and start *moving* on," she said. "Sorry to hurry you, but time is running out. I suggest you decide quickly."

"Let's see," Victoria said, compiling a fast mental list of pros and cons. She certainly would feel better if she could write her thoughts down. Finally, trying to sound convincing to herself as well as to Vicky and Dolly, Victoria announced: "We chose to swim then, and we choose to swim now."

"Very well," Dolly said, positioning herself next to the boat and raising her body slightly, creating a small gray island. "Climb aboard and hold on to my fin."

"If we let go of the side of the boat, we'll drown. I know it," Vicky said.

"You've been drowning for years, and you weren't even in the water," Dolly replied. "You're so afraid you haven't even noticed that the downpour has lessened. Life doesn't come with guarantees. You can either *take* a chance or have *no* chance."

As the princess half crawled, half floated onto the dolphin's slippery back, Vicky began to yell. "Watch it, Victoria! We're rocking the boat!"

"It's all right," Dolly reassured her. "Rocking the boat is a natural consequence of letting go and moving on."

Vicky clutched at the dolphin's fin. "I thought you wouldn't give us a ride out of here because of that man and his fish," she said indignantly, trying to straddle the dolphin so as not to slip off.

"I'm simply going to demonstrate correct swimming technique," the dolphin said, gliding effortlessly through the churning water. "Your turn will come soon."

"No rush," Vicky mumbled.

"We do feel pretty secure riding on your back, Dolly."

"The only lasting security is the security of knowing that one can take care of oneself," Dolly said. "Now do you understand why you must learn to swim?"

"Yes," Victoria said. "I understand."

"Good. Lessons of the sea have much to offer one who is traveling the path. I suggest you pay close attention."

Dolly slowed almost to a standstill. "You will succeed by working in accord with natural forces. That means working in concert with the current, rather than struggling against it. Let go. Go with the flow. Become one with it. Give yourself to the sea."

"We almost did that already," Vicky said.

"I'm glad to see you have a sense of humor, Vicky," Dolly said, quite pleased. "Having a sense of humor makes lessons easier to learn. Now before you can swim, you must first learn how to float. It's like learning to walk before you run. Notice how relaxed I am, how still, how the water supports me without effort on my part. Now lie flat on your back and let me hold you up. I'm going to lower myself farther into the water so that your body is barely skimming the surface. I'll be right below you so you cannot sink."

"On our back? We won't be able to do it," Vicky predicted.

"Distrust of your ability will hold you back and cause you to fail," Dolly replied.

Slowly the dolphin dipped lower and lower into the water. The princess tried to follow her step-by-step instructions, but Vicky became panicky. Many times, Dolly had to raise herself to lift the princess out of the water, reassure her, and repeat the instructions. But Victoria was as determined as Vicky was frightened. She did as Dolly suggested even though Vicky continued to be difficult.

"I can't relax. I can't," Vicky insisted.

"Take some deep breaths and let them out slowly. Feel your mind and body slowing down, relaxing. Going with the flow."

"But how am I s'posed to relax with the sea all choppy and pulling and pushing me around?"

"Stilling one's mind in the face of turbulence is a difficult lesson to learn, but an important one. One will seldom feel peaceful if peace always depends upon finding oneself in calm seas. It helps to concentrate on what you *can* do, rather than on what you *cannot* do. Now begin breathing slowly and deeply," Dolly coached in a calming voice. "Feel your mind and body slowing down."

In spite of Dolly's expert guidance, every time she slipped lower into the water to allow the princess to get a sense of buoyancy, Vicky became frightened and wildly threw her arms about and tried to stand up. Over and over again Dolly had to remind her to breathe slowly and deeply, coax her mind and body to relax, and concentrate on what she could do rather than what she could not.

After a while, Vicky cried, "I'm not strong enough to

do this anymore!"

"There is great strength in surrender. Keep trying."

But again and again, Vicky became frightened and threw her arms about and tried to stand up.

"It's always easier to keep doing what one is doing, even if it doesn't work," Dolly said patiently. "Remember to breathe."

"You sound like someone else we know," Victoria said. "Have you ever heard of an owl named Henry Herbert Hoot, D.H.?"

"Yes, of course. As a matter of fact, Doc and I often work together. We've become good friends. Now that you mention it, he hasn't come by for quite some time."

"You mean Doc comes here? I wonder why he didn't show up when we needed him. He always seems to know everything that's going on."

"He leaves matters of the sea to me, as I leave matters of the heart to him. Now, we must get back to the opportunity at hand."

"Opportunity? *Some* opportunity," Vicky muttered, thinking Dolly sounded as if she had spent too much time around Doc.

"The sea and life have much in common," Dolly continued. "Relax. Let go. Believe it will keep you afloat—and it will. But fight it, believe it will suck you down—and it will. The choice is yours."

After many attempts and repeated reassurances from Dolly, the princess finally floated triumphantly on the surface.

"Excellent! You are now ready to turn over and float facedown," said Dolly.

At first, Vicky fussed about putting her face in the water, but soon the princess was floating as effortlessly on her stomach as she had on her back.

Dolly was delighted. "Now you must learn how to

propel yourself through the water," she said, demonstrating her best style. "Notice the fluidity of my motions. No fighting, no struggling, no flailing of my fins or tail. It's a smooth, regular, consistent effort."

Vicky refused to move. "I wanna believe that the water'll hold us up like you say, but every time I even think of moving, I feel like we're gonna sink."

"You won't believe you *can* do it until you *do,* do it," Dolly said. "You will find that many things are like that."

The princess cautiously lifted her arm into the air as Dolly instructed, but she lost her buoyancy, and Vicky began to slap her hands against the surface and kick fountains of water into the air. "That's it!" Vicky said. "We've learned all we can. We give up, right, Victoria?"

Although drained and frustrated, Victoria had no intention of giving up. She heard Doc's voice in her head as if he were at her side. "Remember what Doc told us, Vicky: 'One gives up out of hopelessness, but one gives in out of acceptance.' We must never give up, only give in. We must accept our fear and do it anyway, or we'll never learn to swim. Come on, Vicky. It's the only way we'll ever get back onto solid ground."

The moment Vicky finally agreed, the tension drained from the princess's body. Slowly she raised one arm, then the other, rounding them into arcs that gracefully cut through the water. The sea smoothed out like glass beneath her. The princess became one with the sea.

"Nature is very giving to those who obey its simple rules," Dolly said, observing the princess gliding through the water. "But it shows no mercy whatever to those who break them. Nature asks little, but its punishment for disobedience is harsh. When one lives in harmony with nature, life flows. Can you feel it?"

"Yes, yes. I feel it!" Vicky cried.

The drizzle stopped, the dark clouds parted, and the

sun came shining through.

"Look! A rainbow!" Vicky squealed, peeking upward at the clear sky between arm strokes. "I'm so glad those dark clouds and all that awful rain are gone."

"It takes both sun and rain to make a rainbow, Vicky," Dolly said. "A fact well worth remembering."

The princess stopped, lifted her head, and paddled lightly in the water. In all the excitement, she had forgotten that she still had no idea which way to go. She looked in one direction, then another.

"I can't see land for the water," Victoria said, feeling her sense of calm fading fast.

"Is that like not being able to see the forest for the trees?" Vicky asked.

Victoria smiled. "Why, Vicky, you sound like me!" she exclaimed, her eyes drawn back to the rainbow. It seemed to be calling out to her. She tried to figure out where the feeling was coming from and why she had it, but she couldn't. Then she decided it was ridiculous to have such a feeling about a rainbow. But the feeling persisted. Finally, she told herself she was probably imagining it. But the feeling was still there.

"Could you tell me if I'm supposed to swim toward the rainbow for some reason?" she hesitantly asked Dolly.

"Why look to others for answers that are in your own heart?"

Her mind flashed back to the time she was beckoned to the little tree on the hill beyond the palace gardens. That was the day she had so desperately needed to find Doc. And he had been there. Now she needed to find land. Could it be that someone was trying to tell her something?

She stared into the rainbow once again. Her heart began to pound as her eyes locked on the band of red. It was the exact shade of her beloved roses! "That is the way I will go," she announced to Dolly.

At that moment a distant spot of land appeared. Victoria was astounded. "Where did that come from? It wasn't there before!"

"Yes, it was," Dolly replied.

"Then why couldn't I see it?"

"Because fear and doubt make one blind to the obvious."

"You mean it was there all the time, but I couldn't see it because I was too afraid?"

"Yes. And you doubted your heart's answer."

"I don't understand. Doc once said that I couldn't see the Path of Truth because I wasn't ready to see it. You say that I didn't see the land because I was too afraid and full of doubt. So is it not being ready or being afraid and full of doubt that makes someone unable to see?"

"Both. When one is fearful and full of doubt, one isn't ready."

"I see how you and Doc became good friends. You have a lot in common," Victoria said.

"Will you come with us, Dolly?" Vicky asked.

The dolphin's head glistened in the sun, her face was bright and smiling. "You must get onto firm ground on your own. And I must be available for the next traveler struggling to keep from drowning."

"We'll miss you, Dolly," the princess said.

"Those you carry in your heart are forever near," said Dolly, fluttering her eyelashes. "I'll remember you always."

With that she turned, waved good-bye with her tail, and slowly disappeared beneath the surface of the water.

The sea was calm. Welcoming. Full of hope. The princess cast her gaze upon the sparkling waters and rejoiced, knowing she could make it to solid ground on her own. A sudden surge of power rose within her, and a sense of peace washed over her as did the gentle waves across her back.

Chapter Twelve

The Land of Illusion

S the princess awoke, she felt the firmness of warm sand beneath her. Never had sand felt so good. She slipped her fingers into it and grabbed a handful. It felt real. Apparently she had made it safely to shore.

Her mind drifted back to the moment she had first spotted land. She had thought her troubles were over, but the swim had turned out to be an arduous endurance contest. By the time she had reached the breakwater, her little remaining energy was completely spent. She couldn't swim another stroke. She had come so far. What if she couldn't make it the rest of the way? Fear had begun to bubble up inside her.

Fear and doubt make one blind to the obvious, she had remembered Dolly telling her. . . . *The obvious.* Could there be a solution her fear and doubt were keeping her from seeing? she had wondered.

That's when another of Dolly's lessons had come to her: *Calming one's mind in the face of turbulence is a difficult lesson to learn, but an important one.* Especially if the turbulence is felt inside oneself, the princess thought. Surely that had to be the worst kind. She had always believed there was no escape from it. But she trusted Dolly's wisdom. She remembered to breathe slowly and deeply to calm herself. She relaxed and went with the flow.

And when she did, the current had washed her ashore. Too exhausted to move, she had fallen fast asleep.

Now, she breathed in the cool salt air and listened to the sea methodically splashing onto the sand.

"I'm too young to be all washed up," Vicky said playfully.

"You're becoming quite a comedian," Victoria replied, suddenly reminded of the prince. How she missed his wit and humor. How she missed *him*. She wished she could have told him that she had finally learned to swim. He would have been so proud—at least at one time he would have. She tried to dismiss the thought with a sigh, but thoughts of the prince were not easy to dismiss.

All at once banjo music rose above the crashing of the waves, and a voice began to sing:

> When you see a lovely rainbow
> Peak through the skies of gray,
> It's a gift from way on high
> To guide you on your way.

"Doc! It's Doc!" the princess shrieked, quickly sitting up and seeing the owl perched on a nearby sand dune.

"Hello, Princess."

"What're you doing here?" she asked, happy to see him.

"Waiting for you. Dolly asked me to deliver this," he replied, holding up a somewhat weather-beaten paisley bag. "She thought you would want it."

"Yes, of course I want it! I can't believe she found it. I lost track of it when I was swept away and dumped into the sea. I thought it was gone forever."

The princess eagerly took the bag and pulled it open. "Everything is probably ruined," she said, "but I'm still glad to have it. Some of my favorite things in the world are in here."

She reached in and pulled out her precious little glass slippers with her initials etched on them. They were still wrapped in the soft wool scarf. Anxiously, she untied the ribbon, removed the slippers, and turned them around and around, examining them closely. "They aren't even cracked!"

"Dolly said she noticed the bag bobbing along on a piece of driftwood in the sea and knew it must be yours. The contents dried out rather well and remained in good condition—considering. Apparently, so did you, for that matter."

"I must look better than I feel," the princess said. "You told me I'd feel better when I started learning about truth, but you never warned me that I might drown trying."

"Feeling as if one is drowning is an opportunity to learn about truth."

"Funny— That's sort of what Dolly said."

"Not surprising," Doc replied. "Truth has many teachers."

"Remember when you told me that truth is the purest, most potent medicine in the universe? Well—are you sure?"

"Yes, Princess. I am sure. Why? Are you beginning to doubt its healing properties?"

"It's just that I've learned quite a bit, and it hasn't worked the way I thought it would. I still shake inside a lot, and my stomach churns and my chest tightens."

"Do you remember what your prescription said? Perhaps it would be helpful to reread it."

"I don't have to. I remember exactly what it says: 'Truth is the best medicine. Take as much as you can, as often as you can.' But I've taken a lot already. I didn't know it would be so hard to take or that it would feel as though I had taken so much for so long."

"I never promised that it would be quick or easy. Only

that it would work." Doc's face softened into a reassuring smile. "Don't get discouraged, Princess. You're making splendid progress, although you may not yet be aware of it."

He put his banjo and straw hat back into his black bag. "Oh, I almost forgot," he said, pulling out a small package of nuts, seeds, and shiny green, red, and yellow fruits and vegetables. "I thought you might want this."

"Thank you. It looks delicious."

Doc gave the package to the princess and zipped his bag shut. "You're very welcome, and now I must leave. I have patients waiting— Ah," he said, delighted. "That's what *you* need—patience and waiting."

"Everyone's a comedian lately," the princess mumbled, memories of the prince beginning to stir within her again.

"You had better get started, too. You have a long way to go. I'll check in on you again," Doc said, rising gently into the air.

"Wait, Doc, please. I don't even know where I am! How do I get back on the Path of—"

But the owl was already airborne. The princess strained to hear his voice over the roar of the waves as he called back to her. "You're still on it. Remember—follow your heart."

"I'd rather follow a map," she muttered, frustrated that Doc had left without telling her which way to go or at least helping her to decide which way.

"A map," she repeated to herself. "If only— Why, of course. The Royal Family Map!" She grabbed her paisley bag and rummaged around until she found the rolled parchment, all the while hoping the ink had not been washed off. She pulled it out, slipped off the silver band, and unrolled it. It was still legible. Relieved, she studied it intently until she figured out which way to go. Then she pulled a small green apple from the package of food Doc had given her and put the rest in her paisley bag, dropping the map on top. She finished the tart treat in short order, then picked up her bag and set out across the soft sand.

Walking was extremely difficult as the princess's feet sank in the sand up to her ankles with each step. After a while it took great effort to continue on. She stopped often to rest and to consult the Royal Family Map, determined to avoid taking even the slightest chance of getting lost.

Vicky was alternately a nuisance and a blessing. She got upset and cried and carried on. She complained endlessly about Victoria not paying enough attention to her, as she was always either charting their course on the map or trying to figure out how their fairy tale had gone wrong. But with it all, Victoria was glad Vicky was there, for it would have been an unbearably lonely journey without her.

As the princess trudged on, the sound of the waves and the smell of salt air faded. The sand turned to gravel, and the gravel turned to blankets of pebbles that rolled beneath her feet, making it necessary to concentrate on every step she took.

"Doc told us we would find blankets of pebbles on the Path of Truth, but he didn't tell us what to do about them," Victoria said, struggling to maintain her balance.

"If this keeps up, it'll take us forever to get anywhere," Vicky whined.

Ah yes, forever. She and the prince had promised to love each other forever.

"Few things last forever, Vicky." Few things, she thought sadly, except the wondering what had gone wrong. And the blaming. And the guilt. And the frustration. And the anger. And the emptiness. And the missing him. And the mourning of the end of her beloved fairy tale.

"Why'd we leave home, anyway?" Vicky asked. "I keep forgetting 'xactly."

"How can you possibly forget such a thing?"

"It's easy. Whenever I think about the prince, all I 'member is how nice and sweet and good and wonderful he was, and I miss—"

"What about how mean and bitter and bad and cruel he was?"

"That's the part I have trouble 'membering."

Victoria sighed. "I don't know, Vicky. Maybe it'll get easier in time," she said, clearing away the pebbles from a spot on the ground so she could lie down.

"It's been a long time already."

"I know," Victoria said sleepily, curling up on the ground and nestling her head in the crook of her arm. "It's getting dark. Go to sleep now."

♥ ♥

The next morning the princess set out once again upon her journey. Before long she came upon a forked dirt path. She stopped and peered down the trail to the left. It was long and straight, until it lazily twisted up the side of a mountain in the distance. Not too bad, she thought. Then she looked down the path to the right. It was steep and narrow, winding and rocky, with big potholes and overgrown shrubbery and trees. Suddenly the princess had the overwhelming feeling that the path was summoning her. Oh, no! she thought. Not *this* path.

But the path and the rocks, the shrubs and the trees, seemed to be calling her name. Why? she wondered. Why would she feel compelled to take what was obviously the most difficult of the two paths? It didn't make sense. Still, the feeling remained. She decided the feeling was ridiculous, but it persisted. She made up her mind that she didn't really feel it at all—that it was only her imagination. But the feeling kept tugging at her, anyway.

Not wanting to take any chances, the princess opened

her paisley bag and pulled out the Royal Family Map. She felt good knowing she could depend on it to give her direction. After all, it had been relied upon by generations of her royal ancestors. She tilted her head, first one way, then the other, tracing her path with her finger.

"To the left. We go to the left," she announced, rolling up the map and sticking it back in the bag. "Thank heavens!"

Soon after embarking upon the path, the princess noticed that although the ground appeared to be level, she had the distinct feeling that she was going downhill. Curious, she thought. Stranger yet was that at one point she saw a brook ahead and was looking forward to having some fresh mountain water to drink, but when she got to where she had seen the brook, it wasn't there. She could almost hear the queen's voice: *Now, Victoria. You must learn the difference between what is real and what is not. People will begin to talk.*

She walked and walked and thought and thought, but couldn't figure out what was going on with the path any more than she could figure out what had been going on with the prince.

Suddenly the princess bumped smack dab into a huge boulder, apparently sitting right in the middle of the path. She could have sworn it wasn't there until it banged into her—or had she banged into *it*? She wasn't sure. But then, there was a lot she still wasn't sure of.

The longer she was on the path, the cloudier the sky became. She soon lost count of how many times the sun had risen and set since she left the water's edge. She also was not too clear on where she had been or where she was going, as the terrain didn't seem to follow her map. She wasn't sure if not knowing where one was, was the same thing as being lost.

A light fog lowered itself onto the path, bringing with

it a chilling breeze. Her stomach began to churn in an old, familiar way, and she could hear Mr. Hide's voice booming in her head: *Sick every time a cool breeze blows. I'm shaking in my boots, Princess.*

It would be so awful to get sick out here all alone with no Dr. Chuckle to bring her chicken soup, she thought, suddenly feeling melancholy. The fog grew denser, and the princess felt as if she were drowning in it.

"I may drown yet—on land, no less. No one would believe it," she mumbled.

"Feeling as if one is drowning is often a gift," a voice said from the mists. "Didn't Dolly tell you about that?"

"Who said that?"

"Who? Who? I did," the voice said.

"Doc! You scared me!"

"You don't need anyone else to scare you, Princess. You do a great job of that all by yourself."

"Dolly taught me how not to be so afraid, but sometimes I can't seem to help it."

"Old habits die hard."

"Really?"

"Of course. It takes much practice to unlearn old habits and put new ones in their place."

"You're lucky, Doc. I bet you don't have to practice anymore."

"It's not a matter of luck. Why do you think my medical practice is called a practice? There are always new lessons to learn."

"You mean I'll never get done?" the princess asked, distressed at the thought of there being no end to her travail.

"As you learn more and more, the trip becomes easier and easier. And it grows increasingly pleasurable."

The princess was encouraged. "What did you mean when you said that feeling as if one is drowning is often a gift?" she asked, wanting to learn more as soon as possible.

"Wasn't it the immediate threat of drowning in the Sea of Emotion that made Vicky finally willing to learn to swim?"

"Yes."

"Challenges carry within them the gift of learning about truth."

"I'm pretty tired of challenges. This path isn't at all what it looks like. I *could* see some things that *weren't* there. And I *couldn't* see some things that *were* there. It's got me all mixed up."

"I would think by now you'd be used to things not being what they seem."

"What do you mean?"

"One seldom sees things as they *are* in the Land of Illusion."

"The Land of Illusion! How did I end up there?"

"You haven't *ended up* anywhere. As for how you got here, this is where you've been for most of your life."

"I've been wandering around in this fog for years and didn't even know it?"

"Yes. Everyone wanders around in a fog in the Land of Illusion. It doesn't much matter that there's fog, though, for here one is unable to see what's in front of one's face even in the best of weather."

"No wonder I've had so much trouble figuring out what's really going on most of the time. How did I get to the Land of Illusion, anyway?"

"By using someone else's map—in one form or another."

"But this map has guided generations of my royal ancestors," the princess said, pulling the Royal Family Map from her paisley bag and holding up the rolled parchment. "Certainly it can guide me, too."

"The trip is different for everyone. What is the right path for one may not be the right path for another. Only one's heart knows the way. You listened to your heart when you were beckoned to the little tree on the hill beyond the palace garden, and you found me. You listened to your heart when the rainbow called to you, and it directed you toward the shore. But when faced with the forked path, you didn't listen to your heart. Instead, you relied on someone else's idea of which way you should go. That's precisely how one gets lost."

"I'm not really lost if you're here," the princess said tentatively.

"On the contrary, Princess. You are every bit as lost, no matter who is here."

Instantly the princess knew the truth of Doc's words as she recalled all the times she had been lost even when the king, the queen, or the prince had been near.

"So what do I do now?" she asked. "Go back to where the paths forked?"

"That is not necessary, Princess. Many paths lead to the same mountain." Then quick as a blink, he spread his wings and disappeared into the mists whence he had come.

Feeling nervous without her map to rely on, the princess continued along the twisted path that snaked through the Land of Illusion. The fog grew so dense, she almost missed a wooden signpost. She went up close to see what it said, hoping it wasn't another illusion. There, in large black letters, next to the outline of a finger pointing straight ahead, were the words:

CAMPSITE FOR LOST TRAVELERS

Chapter Thirteen

Campsite for Lost Travelers

A CLOUD cover hung over the campsite, making it gloomy and damp, and patches of fog dotted the landscape. There were tents and cabins and what appeared to be a few RCWs (Recreational Covered Wagons). Scattered here and there were clusters of people, oblivious to the squirrels and bunny rabbits playfully scampering around them. The din of human voices was a welcome sound to the princess.

A wooden bungalow stood at the entrance of the campsite. Over the door hung a hand-carved sign:

CAMPSITE OFFICE & INFORMATION CENTER

The princess headed up the few steps and pulled open the screen door. It creaked loudly on its hinges. Inside, a wiry-looking man wearing a green-and-burgundy plaid flannel shirt, his feet crossed on top of a desk, was whittling a piece of wood.

"Hi, there," he said enthusiastically, continuing his whittling. "I'm Willie Burgundy."

"Pleased to meet you," the princess replied, finding it interesting that a man by the name of Burgundy was wearing a burgundy-colored shirt. "What are you whittling?"

"I whittle wooden whistles—for workers, mostly."

"Really?"

"Yeah, they like to whistle while they work. I like to *whittle* while *I* work. That's why they call me Willie the Whittler," he said, taking another long swipe with his knife. "What can I do for you this lovely day?"

"I hardly know where to begin," the princess responded, setting down her paisley bag and wondering if Willie had been so busy whittling that he hadn't noticed how dreary it was outside. "I was traveling the Path of Truth and took a wrong turn and found out that my map wasn't any good— Well, it's a long story, but a friend of mine told me that I didn't have to go back, that I can get to where I'm going this way."

"That explains it," Willie replied in a self-satisfied voice.

"Explains what?"

"How you got here, of course. Lots of folks get lost following somebody else's map. And mostly, they end up here."

The princess didn't want to end up at the campsite. Then she remembered Doc saying that no one ended up anywhere—but she was too polite to mention it.

"I've been traveling a long time, and now I'm not sure if I am where I'm supposed to be."

"A buddy of mine—well, sort of a buddy—told me something once: 'One is usually where one is supposed to be,' that's what he said, he did." Willie folded his knife and stuck it and the piece of wood into his shirt pocket. "The lodging here's pretty good. I'll show you." He rose to his feet. "I just got to stoke this here fire a bit first."

"Thank you, but I don't plan to stay. I have to keep going, looking for truth. And there's a temple—"

"Ah, yes. Other folks've come on the same search, but most of them decide to stay here—at least for a while. Lots end up sticking around for good."

"Why would they do that?" the princess asked.

"The Land of Illusion's a pretty seductive place, if you don't mind my saying, miss. Here, folks only *got* to see what they *choose* to see."

"On my way here I walked a path that looked flat but really went downhill. And I saw a brook that wasn't really there. Do you think I only saw what I wanted to see?"

"Yep. Happens all the time."

"I guess the fog makes it hard to see what's really going on," she said, wondering if she knew herself. Then she remembered Doc saying that people couldn't see clearly here—fog or no fog.

"The fog don't matter much," Willie was saying. "What's important ain't seen with the eyes. Anyhow, the fog around here ain't all in the sky—that's for sure."

"What do you mean?"

"Just that folks here are a bit foggy in the head, too. You know, battling all the time about what is and what ain't. Course they're wasting their time because in the Land of Illusion nobody ever knows for sure what is."

"It all sounds very confusing."

"Yep. Folks are plenty confused around here, all right. It's not only folks that're confused, neither. We got little bunny rabbits that're afraid to hop and birds that're afraid to sing."

"Why?" the princess asked, finding it hard to believe.

"Because they think they can't do it good enough."

"What makes them think that?"

"Comparing themselves with others of their kind. There's always some other critter can jump higher or sing sweeter, know what I mean?"

"But that's ridiculous! What possible difference can it make if one rabbit can't jump as high as another or if one bird's song sounds different from another's? . . ." Or if I can't pull a bow back as far as someone else, the princess thought, wondering how that popped into her mind. Then she began to remember all the other times in her life when she had been afraid to do things because she thought she couldn't do them well enough.

"Makes *no* difference," Willie was saying. "Some folks have tried to tell them that, but they don't believe it. Them little bunnies and birds go around angry with their mothers for having them and the world for not making them better."

"Poor things," the princess said, understanding all too well how they must feel.

"That's not the half of it, miss. We got turtles that think their shells are too big and heavy and that they keep them from doing a lot of stuff."

"But turtles are *supposed* to have shells."

"Try telling that to *them*. They ain't interested. They pull back inside and sulk, hoping nobody can see who's in there."

The princess felt sad for all the little creatures. She wondered why they couldn't understand how unnecessary all their suffering was. Then she wondered why for most of her life, she hadn't been able to understand how unnecessary all of *her* suffering was, either.

"There's more, too," Willie said. "There's lots of caterpillars here that slither around trying to hide their faces because they feel so ugly. They don't have no idea they're already pretty butterflies way inside. Then when they finally turn into butterflies, some still see nothing but their old, ugly caterpillar selves staring back at them when they look in yonder swimming hole. Others forget they ever were caterpillars at all. Get big heads, if you know what I mean. There's no talking to them."

The princess thought about the butterflies that still felt like caterpillars. She remembered that she had felt like a butterfly when she was very small—beautiful and free—but how as she grew up, time and time again, she had seen herself as a caterpillar when she looked into the mirror.

Willie's voice brought her back to the present. He was saying something about an apple tree that was too embarrassed to grow apples.

"Why is that?" she asked.

"Because the trees around it grow pears. The apple tree thinks it's growing the wrong thing."

Suddenly the princess could see the king's finger shaking vigorously in front of her nose, and she could hear him bellowing at her: *You're much too delicate, Victoria! Too sensitive. Too afraid of your own shadow. Such a dreamer. What's the matter with you? Why can't you be like other royal children!*

But that had simply been the way she was. Could she possibly have been meant to be that way all along? Victoria felt sad when she remembered the first time sweet little Vicky quietly mumbled: *I am what I am. And what I am isn't good enough.* How could she possibly have yelled at her and made her cry and kept her locked in a closet when all the poor child had done was to be herself!

A big lump formed in Victoria's throat, and her chest grew tight. Oh, Vicky. I'm so very sorry, Victoria said silently. I didn't know. I didn't realize. . . . What have I done to you?

At that moment the princess heard a loud "ribbit, ribbit, ribbit" coming from outside the open office door. Curious, she leaned out to see what it was. A form slowly took shape in the fog. She could hardly believe her eyes—which she knew was nothing new to her. A man was hopping by on all fours.

"What on earth is he doing?" the princess asked, taking a step out the door to get a better look.

"Oh, that's only the prince. Thinks he's a frog," Willie said casually, strolling onto the porch. "If you think that's strange, you should see the frog that prances around wearing a royal robe and crown. Thinks he's a prince. I told you folks are confused around here. Even the flowers are mixed up."

"The flowers? How can flowers be mixed up?"

"Easy. They feel guilty."

"What could flowers possibly feel guilty about?" the princess asked skeptically.

"About soaking up the sunlight, taking up space, and sucking up all the nourishment they need from the earth."

"Why would they feel guilty about that?"

"Because they think they ain't worth it."

"Don't they know how beautiful and fragrant they are? How much pleasure they bring? I'll never forget all the wonderful hours I've spent in rose gardens."

"Them flowers don't know their own worth."

They aren't the only ones, the princess thought. She looked around at the pockets of people and activity. "I'd like to stay and find out what's going on out there, but I really must get back to my search for truth."

"There's plenty of truth right here."

"Here? Nobody here even knows what it is!"

"That's the point, miss. There's a lot of truth to be found in what it ain't. Come on. I'll give you a tour."

The princess wasn't sure she should stay. Then she remembered what Willie had told her his friend had said: *One is usually where one is supposed to be.* Maybe it's true, she thought, reaching inside the doorway and grabbing the handle of her paisley bag.

"You won't find many happy campers here—though some folks sometimes think they are," he said, leading her down the stairs.

Soon they came upon a monkey standing below a tree that hung limply over the edge of a large swimming hole.

"Kindly let me help you, or you'll drown," the monkey said, scooping a fish from the water and carefully putting it up in the tree.

"What's he doing? He's going to kill that fish!" the princess exclaimed.

"Thinks he's helping him," Willie answered.

"Can't we do something?"

"No need. The fish around here have learned what to do when monkeys try to save them."

"You mean this happens all the time?"

"Yeah. This and worse. If you think monkeys saving fish is bad, you should see what happens when folks take to saving other folks."

"I already know about that," the princess said, remembering how she had tried to help the prince in ways that he claimed he hadn't wanted to be helped.

The princess and Willie watched as the fish quickly wiggled itself free from the branch where the monkey had placed it. It dropped gracefully into the water below and swam away.

"I see what you mean about the fish knowing what to do," the princess said with a giggle.

As the pair continued on around the swimming hole, they came upon a man in a white fishing hat sitting motionless on a log.

"What's wrong with *him*?" the princess asked.

"Don't know for sure. Started doing that one day when he couldn't make up his mind which fishing pole to use. Kept asking everybody who passed, but some folks told him to use one pole, other folks told him to use the other. He couldn't make up his mind whether to use a lure or fresh bait or which side of the swimming hole to sit on, either. He asked folks what they thought, but sure enough, some said lure, others said bait. Some said sit here, some said sit there, and other folks said they didn't know, or didn't care—or both. He started looking real nervous, pacing back and forth a lot.

"Then he took to asking folks if there really was any fish in the water—Land of Illusion, you know. Nothing's for sure. Some said they was positive there was fish. Others said course not. He finally stopped asking folks stuff. Next thing we know, he plunks down on that there log, and nobody's seen him move since. Guess the only thing he could decide by himself was to decide nothing no more."

"Did anyone ever ask him why he thought everyone knew better than he did?" the princess asked, a sliver of a memory nudging her.

"Well, we asked him why he had so much trouble making up his mind. Said he was always real scared he'd pick the wrong thing."

"So what if he did?" she said, feeling sorry for the man. "Would the universe have ground to a halt if he had chosen the black pole over the brown one? Or if he had decided to use a lure rather than fresh bait, and had found out later that it didn't work?"

Memories of sending her maid on horseback with a note to the queen asking what to do about this and that flooded the princess's mind. Then pages of pros and cons flashed before her eyes. An old, familiar discomfort crept up in her. She realized that for much of her life, she, too, had asked others for answers and felt nervous when she had had to make a choice, so afraid had she been of making a mistake.

"He looks more like a statue than a man," the princess said.

"Oh, he's a living, breathing man all right. If you walk up close, you can see his breath coming out like a stream of steam in the cold air."

"He may be breathing, but that certainly isn't living! He must be so unhappy," the princess said, her sorrow growing—sorrow not only for the forlorn man before her, but for herself. As the princess looked at the statuelike man on the log, vivid memories bubbled up inside her of the confusion, the misery, and the hopelessness that had overwhelmed her all the days she had taken to her bed and refused to move.

"There's lots of unhappy folks here who ain't doing much more living than him. Don't know who they are or what they're doing here. They muddle through one day after another, worrying over one thing or another, doing one crazy thing after another, and trying to make sense of it all. But they never will, because lots of stuff don't make sense in the Land of Illusion. Guess that's why they call it the Land of Illusion."

At that moment a small, white-gloved creature in a black tuxedo with short pants and a cummerbund with a big brass ring of keys hanging from it stepped up to the princess. He bowed formally and presented her with a white envelope as if it were the most delicate of gems. On the front, in classic black script, were the words "Special Invitation."

"What's this?" she asked, looking up. But the little fellow was already gone. The princess tore open the envelope and read the card inside.

"It ain't what it looks like," Willie said.

"What perfect timing!" the princess exclaimed, paying no attention to Willie's comment. "We're invited to a feast, and I'm starving!"

"Sounds like you ain't given much thought to nourishing yourself lately, but then I bet you ain't done that for a long time, huh?"

"How could I? First, I was too busy trying not to drown and then—"

"When one is drowning, one needs one's strength more than ever," Willie stated as if he were quoting from a great tome.

"I suppose your buddy once told you that, too?"

"Yep. How'd you know?"

The princess smiled.

Willie led the way, warning her again that the feast wasn't going to be what she was expecting. But as they approached the party site, the princess became elated. There were long, cloth-covered banquet tables surrounded by dozens of enthusiastic diners. The murmur of festive voices floated over the scene as a group of small, white-gloved, tuxedo-clad waiters served them from silver platters balanced precariously on their little hands and forearms.

"What are those cute little creatures?" she whispered as they approached the nearest table.

"Wicked elves. But these folks think they're good fairies."

She looked eagerly at the fine china plates and crystal stemware with gold rims, wondering what was being served. She took a closer look at one of the guest's plates. Then at the next plate and the next.

"Why, there's no food on those plates!" she said, astonished, as she watched pencil-thin guests repeatedly lifting empty forks to their mouths, chewing politely, and chatting gaily between mouthfuls. "And those people are all so thin!"

"Yep, they're starving to death, but they don't know it. Don't want to hear it, neither."

"I don't understand it. Why do they stay and put up with this?"

"Peek under here," Willie said, lifting the edge of the tablecloth to expose a row of chained ankles the entire length of the table.

It didn't seem possible. "They're chained here? Why do they look so happy?"

"They don't see the chains or the keys that could free them. And they're convinced they're being fed tasty meals in return for their super-duper service to the elf community.

They can't seem to do enough for those little creatures."

The waiters continued to glide back and forth serving with great style from empty platters, their keys swinging to and fro.

"But how can this be?" the princess asked, dismayed.

"Asked my buddy the same question once. I still remember his answer: 'When one has a gnawing hunger but doesn't know the true source of his emptiness, illusions become his master, and he becomes their slave.'"

The princess continued to watch the unbelievable scene as she contemplated what Willie said. Had illusions made her *their* slave? she wondered. Had her own emptiness caused her to believe the prince was a good fairy, when he was really a wicked elf?

"Lots of folks around here trying to fill their emptiness," Willie said, leading her toward a group of campers only a short walk away.

Men and women, young and old, were sitting around in a circle on a bed of sharp rocks. Some were eating berries while others were scooping handfuls of them from a large golden tureen that stood like an idol on a pedestal in the middle of the circle.

"Why are they sitting in such a rocky spot when there's soft grass right over there?" the princess asked, pointing to an area that looked considerably more comfortable.

"They think it's rocky everywhere. That's one of the reasons why they eat them berries."

"They look delicious. Do you think they would mind if I had a few?"

"Better stay away from *them* berries, miss. They make folks numb to a lot more than the rocks they're sitting on."

"What do you mean?"

"These folks do nothing much except stuff down berries and sit there staring off into space. Like them two over there," he said, nodding his head in the direction of two young men sitting cross-legged on a rock pile. "See that faraway look in their eyes? They think they're on a beautiful beach in Honalulee instead of here, lost. I know. I asked one of them one day.

"And look at them guys—the ones with their faces all scrunched up. Worrying themselves sick about running out of them juicy berries. Can't think of nothing else but how they're going to get more. Pretty soon they'll be jumping up and racing all over the place, looking here, looking there. They must be looking for a lot more than berries."

"What do you think they're really looking for?" the princess asked, sensing that somehow she already knew.

"A way to stop hurting, I guess, for one thing. Them rocks cutting into their seats and feet every day got to be awful painful."

A wave of sadness washed over the princess. "Hurting every day can make people do strange things, all right. And so can feeling empty."

The moment she said it, she became aware of the great big empty place inside herself that had driven her to gulp down bottles of relaxer remedy and to shop day after day from opening until closing in the Old Kingdom General Store. She looked at the people around her and felt sorry, knowing that eating berries wouldn't fill their emptiness any better than relaxer remedy or shopping had filled hers.

Willie shook his head as he and the princess walked away. "Too bad. They're wasting their life. It's a crying shame, I tell you."

"Yes. A crying shame," she repeated, feeling she had had more than enough of both—crying and shame. And come to think of it, she'd also had about enough of the hunger she knew was a result of not having eaten for some time.

"Is there anything around here to satisfy my hunger?"

the princess asked.

"Isn't much in the Land of Illusion to satisfy anybody's hunger, but maybe this'll help," Willie said, leading her to a big citrus tree with a few plump oranges dangling from its branches. He reached up, picked a piece of the fruit, and gave it to the princess.

She sat down under the tree and leaned against the trunk, placing her paisley bag beside her. She dug into the peel with her fingertips and pulled off a piece. The pungent aroma made her mouth water. "Is everyone unhappy here?" she asked, eager to bite into the first juicy morsel.

"Some folks'll tell you they're plenty happy. At least they think they are. At least sometimes. There's a whole bunch of them that thinks everything here's beautiful and wonderful. You can always tell which ones they are by them rose-colored glasses they wear."

Willie reached into his pocket and removed his whittling knife and piece of wood and took one short swipe, then another while the princess hungrily ate the orange.

"Funny things, them glasses," he said, glancing up at her. "The folks wearing them run around saying how terrific everything is, but they're frowning most of the time. Ask them why, and they say you're crazy. They're not frowning. How could they be when everything's so beautiful and wonderful?"

"Is that why they stay here? Because they think they're happy?"

"Folks stay here for lots of reasons. Most stick around because they're used to it. In a weird sort of way, they're comfortable with the craziness. Not knowing what's real and what's not. Being able to see only what they want to see. Even with being unhappy or hurting. Anyhow, they don't know what to expect somewhere else. They're afraid it might be as bad or worse than here. So they figure, why go to all that trouble and take the chance?"

The princess understood all too well how easy it was to remain in a place one was used to, even when one was unhappy. Even when it hurt. As she listened to Willie, she realized how much courage it had taken for her to leave everything that was familiar and set out on a journey into the unknown. Suddenly an electrifying serge of strength pulsated through her.

"Surely some people must have left here, haven't they?" she asked, knowing it was time for her to go, too.

"Oh, yeah. The tales fly fast and furious about the land beyond, and some folks get a hankering to go there. The fog keeps a lot of them from seeing the right path, though. They end up on one that leads deeper into the Land of Illusion. Then they're even worse off than they was here."

"I know how to choose the right path," the princess said with conviction.

"Even so, it's a plenty tough trip. Lots of folks turn back when they see how dangerous the path out of here is. They say the Land of Illusion grabs on to folks and won't let them go."

"I already left one place that had grabbed on to me and wouldn't let me go, but I finally managed to break free. I've made it through a flash flood and through storms at sea that nearly drowned me. I've gotten past blankets of rolling pebbles that threatened to knock me down, and boulders that smashed into me when I tried to pass. I've been empty and lonely and frightened and lost. All this and more I have survived," the princess said, surprised by the message of strength her own words conveyed.

"Even if you made it through, you might come running back. Lots of folks do. They tell the most gosh-darn awful stories you ever heard about what they found there."

"Like what?"

"Like what is."

"What do you mean?"

"They found what really *is*. Not what they want things to be or what they think they are or what they feel they might be—but what really, truly is. That's why they call it the Land of Is."

"Why would they run away from that? What really truly is, is truth. Truth that can heal them."

"Folks say the cure's worse than the disease. You should see the ones that come running back, blubbering and babbling about how they never should've gone. Takes a long time to settle them down. Even then, they're never the same."

"I don't want to be the same," she said, thinking of all the things she still needed to know the truth about. Such as whether or not the prince had really been under an evil spell, and if so, who had cast it upon him and why. Who had done what to whom as she had tried to help him. Why the king and queen had insisted she be who they wanted her to be, instead of who she was. And why she had believed for most of her life that who she was, was not who she was supposed to be.

The more she thought about all she still needed to find out, the more eager she was to get to the Land of Is. She grasped the handle of her paisley bag and lifted it from the ground. "I must know what is, and what was, and what will be. And I can't rest until I do."

"Well, if you're dead-set on going . . ."

"I am," she replied, giving Willie a quick, one-armed hug.

He shifted his weight from one foot to the other and sheepishly lowered his eyes. "I thought you'd be one of the folks who'd leave here," he said. "You got a lot of spunk. Sure do hope you make it."

"Thanks for everything, Willie." She took a deep breath, then another, and listened to her heart as it led her out the far side of the campsite.

Chapter Fourteen

The Land of Is

*T*HE ever-present fog hung heavily in the air as the princess left the campsite. Not knowing what lay ahead, she felt nervous as she passed the exit sign. Then she stopped for a moment and surveyed the land. Her nervousness grew as she remembered Willie's words: *The fog keeps a lot of folks from seeing the right path. They end up on one that leads deeper into the Land of Illusion.*

The princess squinted, trying to see through the dense fog. Ahead, she could just make out several paths, and they all appeared to be difficult uphill climbs. She looked around waiting for her heart to show her the way, but all it did was start beating harder as doubts crept into her mind. What if she took the wrong path and never got to the Land of Is? She couldn't bear the thought of never finding out the truth about what is and what was. Then she would never get to the Temple of Truth and find out what is in the Sacred Scroll. She would never find peace and serenity or learn the secret of true love.

Out of nowhere Doc's voice popped into her mind: *Watch carefully for the signposts.*

Of course, the signposts! She looked from one path to another, then another. But there wasn't a signpost in sight. Why? she wondered anxiously. Why couldn't she see any?

She waited, aware only of the dampness that enveloped her and the pounding in her chest. Suddenly she could almost hear Dolly's voice: *Fear and doubt make one blind to the obvious.*

No wonder! she thought. Her fear and doubt were keeping her from seeing the signposts. They were making her heart pound so hard it couldn't show her the way. She ordered herself to calm down, but the more she fought the fear and doubt, the stronger they grew. The stronger they grew, the more fear and doubt she felt.

Then she remembered Dolly's instructions for overcoming fear and doubt at sea. Surely they would work on land, too. She took several deep breaths, and exhaled slowly, coaxing her mind and body to relax. Then she waited calmly for her heart to show her the way.

Moments later her attention was pulled to the path directly in front of her. Her eyes locked on the vague outline of a post, standing tall in the gray-white mist.

"That must be it," Victoria said. Hesitantly she took a few steps forward, then a few more, and found herself beside a wooden post with a sign at the top:

LAND OF IS
STRAIGHT AHEAD

"I'm not sure I *wanna* know what is," Vicky said, as the princess warily headed up the path.

"Vicky! Where have you been? You were so quiet at the campsite," replied Victoria, pushing aside the overgrown shrubbery that scratched her arms and legs as she tried to pass.

"I was busy feeling stuff."

"You're good at that."

"And I s'pose you were busy figuring out stuff and looking for truth. You're good at *that,* right, Victoria?"

"Right, Vicky."

The princess trudged on over bulging tree roots and

dense weeds that obscured the ground. She picked up a fallen branch to push aside the shrubs.

"Victoria?" Vicky said meekly.

"Yes?"

"It wasn't my fault, was it? I mean that the king and queen and prince didn't love me the way I am."

"No, Vicky. It wasn't."

"But *you* didn't love me the way I am, either," she said sadly. "When we were at the campsite, you said you were sorry. Are you?"

"Yes. More than I can say," replied Victoria, a lump forming in her throat. "Forgive me, Vicky. I *want* to love you as you are."

"Why would you, anyway? Nobody else does," Vicky said in a voice that cut Victoria to the quick.

"Because apple trees are meant to grow apples, and turtles are meant to have shells. Because caterpillars are butterflies inside, and birds' songs are all beautiful. It's hard to explain, but trust me. I'm working on it."

As the princess traveled along, the prickly shrubs seemed to be grabbing on to her, trying to hold her back. She pushed her way through, step by painful step, remembering Willie's warning that the Land of Illusion grabbed on to folks and wouldn't let them go. She concentrated hard on clearing the path with her branch and keeping her feet on the flat ground between the tree roots.

"Victoria?" Vicky said in a small, small voice.

"Yes?"

"I think if you can do it, maybe I can, too."

"Do what?" Victoria asked.

"Love me the way I am."

As the princess climbed higher, the mountainside became rocky and the foliage sparse. She could see farther as the fog grew less dense. She hoped that the path would get easier, but it became so steep and the ground was so moist that she kept slipping back. Each time it happened, she grew more frustrated. It seemed that she slipped back one step for every two forward. Many times she considered turning back, but her vision of the Temple of Truth and all that Doc had promised she would find there spurred her on.

Finally, she grew so tired from the climbing and slipping that she completely lost her footing and tumbled, bag and all, into a big, scratchy bush that was sitting precariously on the edge of a cliff.

"Whew! That was close!" Vicky said, peering over the side of the bush into the deep chasm below.

"Yes, it was," Victoria agreed. "I thought for a moment we were going to slide all the way back down."

"All is well," a voice said. "Although backslides are common on the path, one never slips all the way back to where one was before."

"Doc!" Victoria shouted, quickly freeing herself from the prickly foliage and rolling onto the ground. "I have so much to tell you! The campsite was incredible, and you were right—my heart *does* know the way. And I learned how to keep fear and doubt from— Oh, Doc. I hardly know where to start!"

"How come you're not singing and playing your banjo and wearing your straw hat?" Vicky blurted out, sounding disappointed. "You always sing and play when you first show up."

"Life is too short to *always* do anything," Doc said, "but if you insist. . . ." He whipped his banjo out of his black bag and patted his straw hat onto his head.

There's a wonderful wizard,
Who lives in a land called Is.
When it comes to knowing and growing and such,
The wizard's the best in the biz!

"I wish we could meet him," Victoria said.

"Your wish is about to come true, my lady," Doc replied, bowing, then lifting his hat and tipping it toward the princess in a grand manner.

"Really? A wizard? We're gonna meet a real wizard!" Vicky cried. "What's he like? Will he tell us everything we wanna know? Can we meet him right now?"

"The wizard is sure to amaze you—in more ways than you can possibly imagine," said Doc, smiling mischievously.

"Is he coming here?" Victoria asked.

"No, you're going there—to the Land of Is."

"I've heard of it, but I don't know where it is."

"It's on top of the mountain," Doc answered. "You're almost there. Now be on your way, for the most exciting part of your journey still lies ahead." He lifted off, rising high into the air. "Keep up the good work!" he called. Then he disappeared from view.

Excited about meeting a wizard and knowing that the Land of Is was near, the princess jumped to her feet, pulled her bag from the bush, and set out once again on the Path of Truth.

But before she could reach the mountaintop, the climb took its toll. She was exhausted, and every part of her seemed to ache. Finally, unable to take another step, she slumped to the ground and fell fast asleep before her head even hit her paisley bag.

When the princess awoke, her energy was renewed, and she was eager to get started again on her journey.

"Listen, Victoria," Vicky whispered.

"To what?" Victoria whispered back.

"To the quiet. No one's yelling at us. It's weird, isn't it?"

"Yes, it is," Victoria replied, listening to the silence and remembering. "And it's quiet inside us, too."

After a moment, Vicky spoke again. "Victoria?"

"Yes?"

"Why do we still shake most of the time and churn and tighten? Mr. Hide hasn't been around for a long time."

"I'm not sure. I guess we're used to doing it. Maybe the truth in the Land of Is will heal us, like Doc says."

The princess grabbed her paisley bag and hurried the rest of the way up the mountainside. But on the misty mountaintop nothing looked any different than it had in the Land of Illusion. She was both disappointed and relieved—disappointed because she was eager to find the truth of what is and what was, and relieved because Willie's warnings had her awfully nervous about what might happen to her when she got there.

Suddenly the sun broke through the mist, and a ray of light shone directly on a large signpost a short distance in front of her. That must be it, she thought. Quickly she walked over to the signpost and read:

WELCOME TO
THE LAND OF IS

"Well, here we go again," she said to herself, thinking that maybe the sun greeting her was a good *sign* in itself—then realizing what a clever notion that was.

The princess looked down the other side of the mountain. The Land of Is seemed pleasant enough. The air was clear, and the gentle, moss-covered downhill slope was inviting. The princess couldn't understand why the people Willie told her about had gotten discouraged and gone running back to the Campsite for Lost Travelers. She knew that *she* wouldn't run back, no matter what she found here. Then she thought about the people who had not made it to the Land of Is at all. She had never thought of herself as a strong, determined person, yet it had required great strength

and determination to come as far as she had. It was odd
thinking of herself in this new way, but it felt good.

As they walked along, Vicky kept asking when they
were going to meet the wizard, and Victoria kept answering
that she didn't know.

The princess came upon a large, flat, smooth rock and
gratefully sat down. She opened her paisley bag and
rummaged through it, pulled out her recipe book, and held
it lovingly in her hands. She stared at her name in big
letters under the title, then flipped through the pages,
remembering how many times she had doubted that she
could really write a book and get it published and recalling
all the thinking and planning and testing of recipes it had
taken to finish it.

She reached into the bag again and took out the glass
slippers etched with her initials that the producer of
Cinderella had given her. She remembered how she hadn't
believed she was good enough to get the part, then when
she had gotten the part, that she was not good enough to
play it well. She felt proud of the things she had done. It
occurred to her that she had a right to feel proud. She had
earned that right. The thought was strange to her. Could it
be, she wondered, that the Land of Is was affecting her
somehow?

After returning her book and slippers to the paisley
bag, the princess started off again on her journey, saddened
by powerful memories of the prince and how in their early
days together he had encouraged her and believed in her
even when she hadn't believed in herself. She sighed. If
only he could have stayed as he was then—everything
would have been so different. More than ever, she had to
learn the truth about why he had changed.

It still didn't seem possible for him to have become the
monster he had. When she thought of him—all he had been
to her, done for her, the sound of him, the smell of him, the

feel of him, his smile that made dimples in his cheeks, the way his eyes sparkled just for her, the special way he squeezed her hand gently to silently say "I love you"—the pain still seared into her like a hot poker. But whenever she thought of him, the churning in her stomach and tightening in her chest came back as well, reminding her of all the cruel things he had said and done since that magical day he first approached her in the university library.

"Maybe the wizard will know what happened to him," Vicky suggested.

At that moment a puff of billowy white smoke startled the princess. She tripped and tumbled over and over, coming to a stop, upright, under a signpost. She looked up and read:

TAKE A TRIP DOWN
MEMORY LANE

"That's very funny," Vicky said, having thoroughly enjoyed the tumble down the soft slope. "A *trip* down Memory Lane."

But Victoria wasn't in any mood for having smoke blown in her face and tumbling downhill. "*Some* trip," she grumbled.

"I bet it's the wizard!" Vicky exclaimed. "Don't they usually show up in a puff of smoke?"

But the only one standing there was a small grandmotherly woman wearing a yellow shirtwaist dress and Mother Hubbard shoes that she had apparently dyed yellow to match. "Oh, my!" she said in a lively voice. "Are you all right?"

"Yes, I guess so," the princess said, wondering where the woman had come from. "Just disappointed."

"Why, dear?" she asked.

"Because I thought—well, a puff of smoke made me

trip and fall down here, and I thought the Wizard of Is was about to appear. I guess I was wrong."

"Undoubtedly sometimes you are," she replied. "But not this time."

"What do you mean?"

"I mean that you are correct. The smoke was meant to announce the arrival of the Wizard of Is."

"So where is he?" the princess asked, looking all around.

"He is *me,*" the woman answered, sounding quite amused.

"What? You can't be the Wizard of Is! You don't even have a beard!"

"Many people say that. That's why I bring this along," she replied, whipping a long, gray, matted hairy thing out of her overstuffed, no-nonsense pocketbook and dangling it in front of the princess.

The princess looked at her in disbelief. If this woman was a wizard, she was a sad excuse for one. She couldn't even appear properly in a puff of smoke.

"What about the smoke?" the princess asked.

"People expect it."

"I don't think they expect to have a big puff of it blown right at them."

"Actually, I was training one of my apprentices to execute the technique. Apparently he needs more practice. I'm truly sorry. Can you find it in your heart to forgive us?"

"I guess so," the princess said somewhat reluctantly.

"I'm ever so glad you said that," the woman replied. "It'll be good practice for you, dear. Now that we have all that out of the way, may I formally welcome you to the Land of Is."

"Thank you, but—are you absolutely sure you're the Wizard of Is?" asked the princess, still not convinced.

"Of course I am. I have all the proper credentials. Let me show you." She pulled a fistful of papers from her bulging handbag and thrust an official-looking card at the princess. "Here's my identification card with my picture on it."

The princess examined the card closely. She couldn't believe what she saw. Right under the woman's picture were the words "Official Title: Wizard of Is" and "Address: Land of Is."

"And here's proof of my certification as a current, active board member of the National Association of Wizards. In fact, last year I served as president. Would you like to see the rest of these?" she asked, holding out the remaining documents.

"No," the princess replied. "I'm sorry I doubted you. But I thought wizards were—well, you know."

"Yes, dear. I know. It's all right. People who are new here usually have trouble with reality."

"What do you mean, 'trouble with reality'?"

"Simply that many have preconceived notions of how and what things are or are supposed to be—or were or will be, for that matter, but we'll talk about that another time. Anyway, those notions get in the way of their seeing what really is. Sometimes the condition is quite serious. I have had people refuse to accept that I'm the Wizard of Is even after examining all my credentials and witnessing elaborate demonstrations of my powers."

The princess thought for a moment. "I came a long way to learn what is and what was, and I'm not about to let anything get in the way of my finding out."

"Excellent. Then you will find the truth you seek."

Finally accepting that she was in the company of a bona fide wizard, the princess blurted out the questions that had been plaguing her. "Why have I always been so delicate? So sensitive? So afraid of my own shadow? Such a dreamer? And who cast the evil spell on my Prince Charming?" On and on she went, at full speed.

The wizard listened intently until the fast and furious flow of questions slowed enough to give her the opportunity to speak. "One can never learn the truth from another," she said. "One must discover it for oneself. I trust Dr. Hoot has previously explained that to you?"

"You know him, too?" said the princess. "He sure does get around." She sighed in frustration. "I thought for sure that once I'd found you I would learn the truth about what is and what was."

"You will, dear. But your notions of how wizards work are as erroneous as your notions of what they look like. Wizards are dedicated to helping people see the truth for themselves. Speaking of which, you have a theater performance to attend. Now come along."

"A theater performance! I love the theater. I once played *Cinderella*."

"Yes, I know. You performed exceptionally well. And that wasn't the only time. Come with me. You'll see what I mean."

The princess stood up, grabbed her paisley bag, which had taken the tumble with her, and headed alongside the wizard down Memory Lane.

Chapter Fifteen

A Trip Down Memory Lane

AS she and the wizard walked down the cobblestone lane, the princess felt as if she had stepped into another time and place. Quaint wooden structures lined the path, sprays of untrimmed ivy trailing down their walls. They were separated by welcoming grassy patches and partially shaded by giant, spreading chestnut trees.

"Everything on this street has been painstakingly designed to help people find the truth of their past," the wizard said. "I am sure you will find it ever so unique."

First they came upon what looked like an old country store. "This is Ye Olde Family Business," announced the wizard in tour-guide fashion.

"What kind of business is it?" the princess asked.

"Artifacts—ancient artifacts. They are of great interest to many who visit here."

Next was a rustic structure with a balcony and a large oak entry door. The mass of ivy on the front walls had been trimmed back to reveal a sign that read:

MEMORY LANE INN

"People *stay* on Memory Lane?" the princess asked, concerned that maybe this was going to take longer than she had thought.

"Yes. For as long as they need to."

"How long is that?"

"For some, a short time. For others, longer. The only ones we worry about, though, are the few who become reluctant to leave. They require extra attention, as getting stuck in the past is a serious matter."

What came next was unmistakably a playhouse, complete with a billboard sitting on a large wooden easel announcing the current play.

—YE OLDE LEGACY PLAYHOUSE PRESENTS—

PUPPETS OF THE PAST
A Saga to Remember

—

Starring PRINCESS VICTORIA
with
The King, the Queen, and the Prince

The princess was stunned. "*I'm* starring in this play! You said I was going to *see* a play, not be *in* one!"

"This is a replay of the original production in which you've been starring for all your life. It will explain all that *was,* and all that *is* because of all that *was.* We must hurry along now. It's time to begin."

But the princess just stood there, staring at the ground.

"What's the matter, dear?" the wizard asked.

The princess shuddered. "What if—what if I find out— I mean I've waited so long, what if—"

"In the Land of Is, there is no what *if.* There is only what *is.* And what *is* hurts worst when you *don't know* what it is."

"I hope I like the things I find out," the princess said nervously.

"Most likely, you will like some parts of the truth and dislike other parts. Some parts you will love, others you may hate. But good, bad, or indifferent, what is, is. And your not knowing the truth doesn't change it. It only gives it the power to run your life without any interference from you."

"Do I really have to do this?" the princess asked.

"Life is lived looking forward, but it's understood looking backward. You've waited a long time to understand. The choice is yours."

The princess inhaled deeply and nodded to the wizard, who gently took her hand and led her into the playhouse.

"Now, dear," the wizard said, sitting down next to the princess. "There is one more important aspect to this unusual production that you should know about. You will not only see the action and hear the dialogue, but you will also be aware of what the people are thinking and feeling."

"You mean I'll hear what's going on in their heads?"

"Yes, and feel what is going on in their hearts."

The wizard snapped her fingers, and the playhouse darkened. "Let the play begin," she called out, spreading her arms and raising them high in the air. A puff of white smoke filled the stage and quickly dissipated, revealing a wooden easel with a sign on it that said "Act I."

The wizard snapped her fingers again, and a little girl appeared onstage, looking lonely and sad. The princess recognized her immediately from the painting that hung on the sitting room wall in her parents' palace. It was the queen when she was a child. The princess was amazed to see her mother's life being played out before her eyes. And it felt strange to know everything she was thinking and feeling.

The princess watched scenes of the little girl growing up. She saw her with her parents and with friends. She saw her at home and at school. She experienced her hopes and her dreams, her fears and her doubts. The princess laughed and felt her joy. She cried and felt her pain. As Act I drew to a close, the princess understood for the first time how the queen had become the kind of woman, ruler, wife, and mother that she had.

With a snap of the wizard's fingers, a new billboard appeared on the easel announcing Act II. The princess immediately got caught up in the trials and triumphs of a little boy, who she knew was the king. She shared in his happy times and in his sad ones. She worried when he worried, hurt when he hurt, and rejoiced when he rejoiced. Before long the princess understood how the king had become the man, ruler, husband, and father that he had.

Act III opened with the queen holding her newborn princess in her arms, the king affectionately looking on. As the scenes continued, the princess reexperienced many moments of her life—some so painful she quietly sobbed through them. Some scenes were exactly as she remembered them. Others were somewhat different. Still others, she had completely forgotten. She saw Vicky in all her splendor and innocence. She saw her in all her darkest moments. By the end of Act III, the princess understood how she had become the woman, daughter, and wife that she had.

The princess was relieved when there was finally an intermission. She was too overwhelmed with sadness to watch anymore. As she and the wizard talked, sad turned to mad. But being mad wasn't easy with the Royal Code of Feelings and Behavior for Princesses raging in her head. Back and forth the princess went from mad to sad and back again.

Finally, with some prodding from the wizard, the princess cried out that she was angry with her parents and everyone else in her life who had told her that she wasn't okay as she was. And she was angry with herself for believing them. She felt guilty for being angry. And she felt angry that she felt guilty for being angry. Every now and then her mind went numb, and she would forget for a moment what she and the wizard were talking about.

The wizard said it was all perfectly understandable for a princess who had followed the Royal Code since childhood to judge what she was feeling, and that it was no small matter for any royal child to witness the king and queen topple from their royal pedestals and fall to the ground like lowly commoners.

"But maybe they couldn't help what they did to me," the princess said, remembering her parents' past and feeling guiltier than ever for blaming them for the way they had treated her.

"It's true that people do the best they can at the time with the tools they have and the pain they have," the wizard answered. "And having compassion for them is fine. It opens the door to having compassion for yourself as well. But know that what happened to you was not okay. And no reason—no story—could ever be good enough to excuse your being discounted, made to doubt what you thought and believed, and forced to deny what you felt. And nothing you ever did made you deserve it."

The pain, anger, guilt, and sadness continued to swirl through the princess like a mighty tornado. "Where did all these feelings come from?" she asked.

"Most times, people's feelings have the same roots as they do."

After that, the princess cried and cried, until finally spent, she slumbered in the wizard's arms.

♥ ♥

"Wake up, dear," the wizard said sometime later. "It's time for Act IV."

The princess braced herself for what she knew was coming—the appearance of the child prince. From the moment he appeared onstage, she was fascinated by the tiny boy who was to grow up and become her Prince Charming. Her spirits rose and fell with the highs and lows of his life. She witnessed his challenges and his victories. She felt his struggles, and she saw how he came to joke away his pain. The princess sat riveted to her seat as she witnessed the early beginnings of the evil spell that later changed her cherished Dr. Chuckle into the hideous Mr. Hide.

When Act IV ended, the princess looked intently at the wizard. "It's all so hard to believe. I always thought the *real* prince was my sweet, wonderful Dr. Chuckle and that Mr. Hide was only an evil spell someone had cast on him. I had no idea the real prince was both of them all along."

"Such is the nature of Mr. Hides—and the nature of fairy tales that feel more real than what *is*."

Then with a snap of the wizard's fingers, Act V began. It opened in the university library with the princess looking up into the bluest eyes she had ever seen. Excitement pulsed through her as it had the first time. She relived all the ecstacy and agony of her days with the prince. But this time she understood what was happening and why. Although it was a relief to have figured it out, understanding did not take away the aching, the anger, the sorrow, or the emptiness of being without him.

She and the wizard talked about it until the princess finally screamed out, "I'm furious with the prince for destroying my fairy tale, for betraying my trust and my love."

"Of course you are, dear," the wizard replied compassionately. "And are you furious with anyone else?"

"Yes, with myself!" the princess yelled, shaking her fists in the air. "I'm furious with myself for allowing him to hurt me so deeply for so long."

As she continued to feel what needed to be felt and say what needed to be said, her fury grew until it could grow no more. Then slowly it dissipated, freeing her of the burden that had lain heavily upon her for a very long time.

She thought back to the scenes she had watched of the child prince growing up. "He was angry about lots of things before we even met, and he took it all out on me. I never had a chance. He used the love I had for him to hurt me, and he took pleasure in my pain. But for a long time I couldn't bring myself to leave."

"People become the victim of victims when their need to be loved overshadows their need to be respected," the wizard replied. "Overall, people get what they will settle for. No more and no less."

"Maybe they settle for what they're used to," the princess said, recalling the depth of her love for the king and queen and the depth of the pain that was part of it.

"That's true. People seek what they know. That which is familiar is comfortable."

"Even if it's a struggle?"

"Yes, *especially* if it's a struggle. The times change. The people change. But they are still trying desperately to get it right, work it out, finish up their unfinished business. Unfortunately, they usually try to do it the same way that didn't work the first time."

The princess shifted uncomfortably in her seat. "Is that what the prince was doing? He said he couldn't help turning into Mr. Hide."

"Perhaps, but carrying on a legacy of pain is always a choice—and an irresponsible one at that. Everyone is accountable for his or her actions and is responsible for working through his or her own pain so as not to inflict it on others. The doors of Ye Olde Legacy Playhouse are open to all."

"If only he had come here long ago," the princess said somberly. "Maybe he could have gotten better, and things might've been different."

"Maybe, but some people are too afraid to face what

they must face here and are unwilling to do what they must do."

The princess's brow furrowed. "What a waste. All those years of shaking and churning and tightening, of feeling helpless and confused and sick and tired."

"When you permit other people's judgments to be more important than your own, you give away your power."

"Holding on to power must be easy for you. Your power is so great."

"So is yours, dear. But like all power, it must be recognized and exercised or it lays dormant."

The princess took a deep breath, trying to relax the tenseness in her body. "If I'm so powerful, why do I feel that I still love him, even knowing all that I know?"

The wizard took the princess's trembling hands in hers. "*Knowing* is one thing and *feeling* is quite another. It can take a long time for the feeling to catch up with the knowing. Be patient, dear. It will come."

The princess mulled over all the wizard had said. It was a lot to think about.

Then another question popped into the princess's mind, demanding to be answered: "I loved him with all my heart and soul, but he said it wasn't enough. Why?"

"No ten princesses could have loved him enough to satisfy him," the wizard said. "Often people who feel unlovable—like the prince—doubt other people's love for them. They don't believe love could come to anyone so unworthy as themselves."

Tears began streaming down the princess's cheeks. Faster and faster they came until she was sobbing uncontrollably from the anguish and futility of it all.

Before long, Vicky's shaky, sniffling little voice crept into Victoria's awareness. "We have to be careful not to flood the playhouse," she said. "You know what happened to us the last time we cried this hard. We nearly drowned."

"That was before we learned how to swim," Victoria reassured her. "The water may get deep, but we never have to worry about drowning in it again."

"Lessons well learned bring great peace," the wizard said, stroking the princess's lowered head.

"I wish I could feel peaceful about all that's happened to me."

"You can."

"How?" the princess asked, looking up into the wizard's kind face.

"By being willing."

"Willing? Willing to what?"

"Willing to continue feeling all of your feelings about what happened to you in the past until they lose their power. Willing, this time, to comfort and reassure Vicky through it all instead of blaming her. And willing to forgive yourself for being unable to do any better than what was, at the time, your very best."

The princess dabbed at her eyes with the handkerchief the wizard handed her. "I don't understand why it all had to happen."

"Life is difficult. Some people come into other people's lives and leave footprints on their hearts, and they are never the same. But not being the same can be better."

"What do you mean, 'better'? How can someone be better for having been hurt?"

"Have you not grown wiser about what love is and what it isn't? Have you not learned more about who you are and who you're not? And have you not learned how to summon strength from deep within that you didn't even realize you had?"

"I guess so," the princess answered.

"There is a valuable gift in every relationship, in every experience. The sooner you can see the gift, the sooner you can move through the pain."

"Doc once told me that challenges carry within them the gift of learning about truth. I still don't see why I have to hurt to learn, though."

"Pain is a much better teacher than pleasure. Think of yourself as a person-in-training. Then your experiences become lessons. And from your lessons come wisdom that makes life fuller and richer—and easier."

The princess shook her head. "It sure is a hard way to learn."

"Yes, but it's the way people learn best. And suffering can stretch your heart to make more room for love and joy."

The princess sighed. "Love and joy? I don't know. After all that's happened . . ."

"The way you lived *yesterday* determined your today. But the way you live *today* will determine your *tomorrow,*" the wizard said. "Every day is a new opportunity to be the way you want to be and to have your life be what you want it to be. You no longer have to be stuck in your old beliefs. As you have seen, they come from other people, other times."

The wizard reached out and placed her hands on the princess's shoulders. The look in the wizard's eyes warmed the princess through and through.

"Listen closely, dear. What I say to you now is of the utmost importance." The wizard spoke slowly and determinedly. "The years have passed. The dangers have passed. It is safe to be you."

Chapter Sixteen

The Valley of Perfection

A S they walked out of the playhouse, the princess turned the wizard's words over and over in her mind.

"Are you saying that I don't have to keep trying to be different? That I'm okay as I am?" she finally asked.

"You are better than okay," the wizard replied. "In fact, you are perfect."

The princess hung her head. "That's what I've tried to be all my life. But no matter what I did, I was still too delicate and sensitive and afraid of things and dreamed of things that probably wouldn't ever happen."

"Did it ever occur to you that maybe you were *meant* to be all those things?"

The princess sighed. "Yes. It occurred to me, but I found it hard to believe. I don't really know *how* I was meant to be. Or who, or why."

"It's about time you found out, don't you think? Fortunately, we're headed for the *perfect* place," the wizard said, quickly placing her hand over her mouth to muffle an impish little laugh that managed to escape in spite of her best efforts to squelch it. "Come along, dear. There is something I want to show you."

The wizard led the princess to the top of a large hill. "May I present one of the most spectacular sights on earth—the Valley of Perfection," she said, opening her arms as if to embrace the beauty that spilled over the rolling countryside below them.

"Valley of Perfection? You mean everything down there is perfect!"

"Yes, everything."

Surrounded by the most lush greenery the princess had ever seen was a pond bluer than the prince's eyes. Ribbons of sunlight danced upon the water. Patches of strawberries and clumps of wildflowers grew with abandon, their scents mingling and rising to the hilltop. Squirrels scurried, butterflies fluttered, and the sweet song of meadowlarks rang through the air. Everything looked fresh and clean, as though it had been washed by a gentle rain.

"If only I could be that perfect!" the princess said, in awe of the flawless beauty she witnessed before her. "Can we go down there?"

"Of course," the wizard answered, leading her down the long, gentle slope.

As they walked the princess swept her eyes across the valley. The more she saw, the more she realized that things weren't as perfect as they had appeared from the hilltop—and the more she realized it, the more disappointed she felt.

"I thought you said that everything in this valley was perfect. I mean, it's nice here, but when you see everything up close, it's not perfect at all. The shrubs don't look as green. The trees are ordinary. The pond isn't as clear. There are bugs and—well, at least *these* still look good," she said, reaching down and picking a plump, bright red strawberry and holding it up to the wizard. "This is the only thing that still looks perfect."

But as she sank her teeth into the scrumptious-looking morsel, her face scrunched up and her mouth puckered. "It's sour! *Nothing* is perfect here. Absolutely nothing."

"You, my dear, are very accomplished at blemishing

the majesty of what is."

"I don't usually. But you said everything here was perfect, and it's not. I'm so disappointed. I expected—"

"Perfection, as beauty, is in the eyes of the beholder."

The princess was puzzled. "But anyone can see that the shrubs and the trees and the pond and the strawberries aren't perfect." She lowered her eyes and mumbled, "But then, maybe nothing is. Not the king or the queen or the prince or me—or even love or my fairy tale."

"All is as it is meant to be," the wizard said reassuringly. "That makes it perfect. What is flawed is your manner of perceiving perfection."

As the wizard continued, the princess only half listened, for she was troubled that even her manner of perceiving perfection was apparently imperfect.

"Rocks are hard and water is wet, and sometimes plump, bright red strawberries are sour. What is, is. In all of nature, everything is and does what it was designed to be and do."

"All I was designed to do was to be imperfect."

"On the contrary, you were designed perfectly to fulfill the universe's plan for you."

The princess shook her head. "I don't know anything about a plan. I only know that I tried to convince myself that I'm okay the way I am, but there are so many things about me I'd like to change."

"The deepest part of you—the part that is one with all—is perfect," explained the wizard. "It always was, and it always will be. Perfection is nature's gift. It is not something you have to earn. It is something you *are,* regardless of the things about you that you think might better be changed."

The princess thought about all the years she had tried to look perfect and do everything perfectly. "You mean I was already perfect the whole time?"

"Precisely! You are a part of all that is. And what is, is perfect in its so-called imperfection."

"But what about my being too delicate and sensitive and afraid of things and dreaming about things that probably won't ever happen? And my lists of pros and cons?"

"When you accept the miracle of who you are and love yourself without condition, changing the things that need changing will come easier. But some of the very things about you that you have always thought needed to be changed—things you believed were your failings, your enemies—have actually been your loyal servants," the wizard said. "It is because of them that you are who you are. A unique, perfect you—unlike any other who has come before or who will follow."

The princess's mind began to race. Could it possibly be true? She thought of all the years she had fought being the way she was. The hundreds, thousands, maybe millions of times she had been angry with herself for not being different, for not being better.

"There were times I thought I wasn't good enough to be loved," she said, her lower lip quivering.

"My poor dear," the wizard said, taking the princess's shoulders in her hands and looking directly into her eyes. "You have always been good enough to be loved. Not because of what you said or did not say, or what you did or did not do, but simply because you are a child of the universe. The time has come to honor that which you have denounced for most of your life."

She took the princess's hand in hers. "It is time to appreciate being as delicate as your beloved roses that bloom in the palace garden. It is time to appreciate the sensitivity that has opened for you the door to the pleasures of the universe, for one who feels the depths of pain also feels the heights of joy. It is time to appreciate your fears, for they have challenged you to develop the strength and courage of a valiant knight in battle. And it is time to appreciate the dreams that speak of your heart's desires, for they are trying to reveal the secret of the universe's plan for you." On and on went the wizard, lovingly pointing out the undeniable truth.

The princess felt as if she were suspended in time and space. Gradually a burdensome weight lifted from her shoulders and floated off. Everything began to take on new meaning. She thought about all she had been through and of all she had learned. She thought of how she had grown and blossomed into who she was now because of all that was before. She remembered it all—and she felt good.

All at once everything in the valley seemed different. Bright rays of sunlight kissed the wonder of all that was. Trees and shrubs turned greener. The pond turned bluer. And the fragrance of thousands of flowers turned sweeter. The princess watched the squirrels scurrying, the butterflies fluttering, and listened to the song of the meadowlarks. Everything seemed as fresh and new as if she were experiencing it for the very first time. Suddenly a feeling of intense love arose in her.

"I feel more beautiful now than I ever have before—except for maybe when I was very small," she said, thinking back and trying to remember.

"When you look for beauty in all that is, you begin to see the beauty in yourself as well," the wizard replied. "If you look for beauty in what is, you will find it. If you look for imperfection, you will find that instead."

At that moment a small, familiar voice intruded upon the princess's thoughts. "Victoria?"

A lump rose up in Victoria's throat. "Yes?"

"I was right about something," Vicky said.

"About what?"

The reply came a moment later. "About being able to

love myself if you could love me the way I am."

Sobs of joy came in waves, as together Vicky and Victoria laughed and cried and cried and laughed, until they were submerged in puddles of happy tears.

"We don't have to worry about drowning this time, do we, Victoria?" said Vicky jubilantly. "We're never gonna drown because we have each other. And we know how to swim. Right, Victoria?"

"Right."

A sense of calm came over the princess unlike any she had ever felt before.

"It feels somehow like I've come home."

"You have," the wizard replied. "To the home and family that you long ago forgot you even had. To the home and family that many people spend a lifetime searching for—never realizing that all the time they were already there."

"Family? What family?"

"In the Land of Is, everything is family, including rabbits and birds and fish and flowers and stars and you and me. From this moment on, wherever you go, wherever you are, will be home, because whatever and whoever you're with will be family."

The princess looked at the beauty that surrounded her—the beauty that she was a part of—and she felt whole.

"Now, dear, the Temple of Truth and the Sacred Scroll await you."

"The Temple of Truth!" the princess cried. "I didn't see it. Where is it?"

"Atop that mountain," the wizard said, motioning toward the other side of the valley. "It's a lovely walk. You will enjoy it."

"Aren't you coming with me?"

"No, this leg of the journey you must take alone."

"But why?"

"Because it is the only way you can hear the voice of the Infinite."

"What's that?"

"The voice of the Infinite cannot be explained. For one to know what it is, one must experience it."

"Will I ever see you again?" the princess asked, beginning to miss the wizard already.

"Of course, dear! Sooner than you think," the wizard answered, blowing the princess a kiss. Then she was gone in a puff of white smoke.

With a light heart, the princess set off across the valley toward the Temple of Truth. When she reached the base of the mountain, she saw a large weeping willow standing like a monument against the late afternoon sky. Although bent under the burden of its great weight, it reached upward with strength and hope. She stood for some time under its boughs wondering why it fascinated her so. Finally she realized what it was. It reminded her of herself—and of all life—as it reached determinedly skyward, turning the weight of its burdens into beauty and grace.

She plunked down her paisley bag and sat beside the tree, leaning her head against the trunk and closing her eyes. She grew so relaxed that after a few minutes even the clamor of her own thoughts drifted away. That's when she heard it.

The voice of the Infinite was like no other. It was a gentle voice that spoke to her heart like a whisper. At first the princess thought she had imagined it.

Softly the voice spoke again. It was not so much what it said that made her think something very unusual was happening, but the feeling she had in its presence. She felt soothed, reassured, and validated. Love seemed to wrap itself around her like a warm blanket in winter.

"Why haven't you spoken to me before?" she asked.

"I have, many times. But you did not hear me," came

the reply.

Questions of great importance then began to crowd into the princess's mind, competing for attention. "I have a million questions to ask you," she said, feeling foolish and uncomfortable, as she was still not convinced that she wasn't simply talking to herself.

"Whatever the question, the answer is truth," the voice said. "Find truth and you shall know all you need to know."

"But what about love?" the princess asked.

"Wheresoever goes truth, goes love."

Undaunted, the princess then asked, "Are truth and love what it's all about? Life, I mean."

The voice of the Infinite graced her with a reply. "Life is all about discovering what life is all about."

Then as mysteriously as it had come, the voice seemed to disappear.

"Wait, don't go! Don't leave me," the princess called out, worried that in its absence she would lose the all-encompassing feeling of love and comfort she felt.

"I am a part of all that is, as you are a part of all that is. I am within you, and you are within me. We are forever together, even as you may think we are apart," the voice said.

The great big empty place that had remained deep within the princess for years filled with contentment, with belonging, and with peace.

"Do you promise?"

Like a distant echo in the wind came the reply: "I will always be there for thee. You have only to call—and then to listen."

The silence that remained after the voice drifted off seemed fuller somehow.

Then the princess headed up the mountain toward the Temple of Truth, her heart thumping with anticipation and her paisley bag swinging merrily at her side.

PART IV

Chapter Seventeen

The Temple of Truth

*T*ime seemed to pass quickly as the princess climbed up the mountainside, her mind filled with curiosity about what wonderful secrets the Sacred Scroll would reveal and visions of the magnificent temple she was soon to behold. But even her most elaborate visions had not prepared her for the spectacular beauty that greeted her when she finally arrived.

As she stood in the warmth of the mid morning sun, peering through the elaborate grillwork of two tall, white wrought-iron gates, they unexpectedly swung open in invitation, revealing the stately structure within. Carved white stone columns, broad, graceful steps, and beveled-glass entry doors that glistened in the sunlight made the temple more stunning than the grandest palace the princess had ever seen. Stretches of plush green grass carpeted the courtyard, and flower beds abundant with lush foliage and bursting with color wrapped the temple in splendor.

She took a deep breath and started out across the courtyard, with large, heart-shaped granite stepping-stones beneath her and fluffy white clouds riding on a gentle breeze above.

A moment later a chorus of whispers rang out all around her. "Grow . . . grow . . . grow," the voices said encouragingly, as if they were speaking to each and every blade of grass, each and every tree, shrub, and flower. The princess immediately recognized the voices as all being one. It was the voice of the Infinite.

Everything was moving, swaying, flowing in the sunlight, pulsating to the beat of the universe. At that moment the princess knew to the depths of her being that Doc and the wizard and the voice of the Infinite had all spoken the truth about who she was and all *that* was.

As she approached the temple, the entry doors swung open. "This is it," she said, stepping inside, her heart racing with excitement.

A three-tiered, white stone fountain stood tall in the center of a large foyer. Crystal clear water cascaded down in shimmering sheets that threw their music into the air. Slowly the princess continued on, her body resonating to the rushing of the falling water.

When she reached the other side of the foyer, she looked into the temple's main room. What she saw took her breath away. Alternating panels of polished white stone and beveled glass formed a massive rotunda. At the far side of the room in front of a wall of solid stone was a large platform on which sat a throne generously draped with velvet the exact shade of the king's royal robe. On each side of the throne was a white alabaster pedestal that held an exquisite, hand-cut crystal vase filled with dozens of long-stemmed red roses. The intense green and array of striking colors from the courtyard came through the glass panels, splashing a garden of hues throughout the rotunda. Shafts of brilliant sunlight beamed down through an enormous beveled-glass dome.

In awe, the princess stepped into the room. "Hello," she called out, wondering who was in charge. Surely someone must be around. "Hello," she called again.

Not knowing what to do next, she wandered toward the throne. She stepped up onto the platform and instinctively went to one of the vases of roses. She leaned close and inhaled deeply. She had always tried to stop and smell the roses, even though for some time she had been unable to fully enjoy them.

She set down her paisley bag and ran her fingers over the throne's soft velvet covering. "Is anyone here?" she called, wondering whom the throne belonged to. Still there was no answer. Feeling tired from her journey, she sank into the mass of velvet, hoping that the person whose throne it was would not mind. She felt as she had as a small child, enveloped in the king's robe when he hugged her tightly, his chest puffing up with pride. She reflected on her journey from then to now. It had been long and difficult, but it had brought her to where she was today, and she was glad she had taken the trip. Then, remembering the Sacred Scroll and realizing she hadn't seen it, she glanced around the room, but the scroll was nowhere in sight.

Abruptly, out of nowhere, a bluebird swooped down and landed on her shoulder. She was stunned. Where had it come from? she wondered. It had been a long time since she had had a feathered friend perched on her shoulder. It felt wonderful. She reached up to the bird and offered her finger. The bluebird hopped onto it. She lowered her hand and looked directly into the bird's face and at its unusually round body.

"Why, I know you! You're the same bluebird that used to fly in through my kitchen window and land in my chopped pistachio nuts!" she shrieked with glee.

The bluebird's eyes seemed to be gleaming, and it began chirping a lively tune.

Suddenly banjo music echoed throughout the rotunda, playing the same tune. The princess jumped from the throne, the chirping bird still perched on her finger.

"Doc! Oh, Doc, am I glad to see you!" she cried. "What are you doing here?"

"I'm accompanying the Bluebird of Happiness, of

course. In more ways than one," the owl replied, continuing to strum the banjo.

"The Bluebird of Happiness? *This* bird?" the princess said, looking with surprise at the chirping creature sitting on her finger. She looked into its eyes again. "No wonder I always felt so good when you showed up, little fellow. I guess it's true that to find happiness, one must look only as far as one's own backyard—or kitchen—as the case may be," the princess said with a giggle.

"True happiness is found neither in backyards nor kitchens," Doc replied. "And it doesn't come from birds—even this one—nor from the other side of the fence where the grass seems greener. It bubbles up from deep inside when one knows the truth of things."

"You mean the bluebird doesn't bring happiness?"

"Like a Prince Charming, the bluebird comes to help one *celebrate* one's happiness. He is not responsible for *bringing* it."

The princess pondered Doc's words as she listened to the melodic tune.

"You make such beautiful music together. The prince and I once made beautiful music together. Oh, how I long to have that again."

"And so you shall one day. But there are other things to attend to first."

"Like the Sacred Scroll? I looked all over and couldn't find it. Whoever's in charge here must know where—"

"*We* are in charge here."

"But—but whose throne is this?"

"Yours, Princess," Doc answered.

Suddenly a huge puff of white smoke appeared. In the middle of it was an animated silver-haired figure waving madly to clear the air.

"I hope I'm on time!" the wizard called out. "I wouldn't want to miss anything."

"You and I both know you never miss a *thing,*" Doc said, winking at her playfully.

"Henry, how nice to see you. And you too dear," she said to the princess. "I see you made it up here just fine, as I knew you would." Turning back to the owl, she asked, "Is everything all set, Henry?"

"Set for what?" the princess asked.

"She doesn't know yet," Doc whispered to the wizard.

"Know what?" asked the princess.

"Know that we've planned a special commencement ceremony for you," Doc replied.

"Really? For me?" the princess said with childlike delight. "Is that when I'll get to see the Sacred Scroll?"

Before Doc could answer, a flock of birds flew into the room chirping noisily and circling around the princess, some briefly alighting on her shoulders and arms.

"My old feathered friends!" she exclaimed, recognizing the birds from days gone by.

One by one, she stroked their little heads with her finger, and one by one they cooed as she did. "I'm so happy to see you again," she said. "I've missed you all so much."

When the princess finished stroking the last bird, the wizard spoke. "Will you please take your throne now, Princess. And all guests please take your places. The commencement ceremony is about to begin."

The birds flew around and quickly came to rest in neat little rows, theater style, facing the throne. The wizard took her place beside it.

As the princess nestled back into the velvet seat, a pigeon—apparently straggling behind the others—flew in with two envelopes in its beak and gave them to Doc.

"What are those?" the princess asked above the twittering of the birds that had started up again when the pigeon flew in.

"They're birdiegrams, of course," Doc answered. "For you. Do you want to read them?" he asked, offering them to her.

"No, you read them so everyone can hear."

All was quiet as Doc opened the first envelope. He cleared his throat, then began to read:

WISH I COULD BE WITH YOU TODAY, BUT CAN'T—FOR OBVIOUS REASONS. HOPE YOUR HAPPINESS RUNS AS DEEP AS THE OCEAN, AS HIGH AS THE SKY. AM WITH YOU IN SPIRIT, ALWAYS. LOVE, DOLLY.

"That was so sweet of Dolly," the princess said. Chirps of approval rang throughout the rotunda. Doc and the wizard said they thought Dolly's sentiments were lovely and sounded exactly like her.

Then Doc opened the second envelope and read:

CONGRATULATIONS. WAS GLAD TO HEAR YOU'RE NOT JUST WHITTLING AWAY YOUR TIME. HOPE YOU CARVE OUT A BEAUTIFUL NICHE IN LIFE.

Doc looked briefly at the princess, then back at the birdiegram. "It's signed: 'Best,' but that was scribbled out. Underneath, it says: 'Sincerely yours,' but that was also crossed out. Underneath that is, 'Aw heck. Love, Willie the Whittler Burgundy.'"

The princess giggled. "Isn't he adorable!"

Doc chuckled and said he thought Willie's birdiegram was clever. The birds broke into a round of enthusiastic chirping and wing flapping. The wizard found it all extremely amusing.

When the chirping, flapping, talking, and laughing waned, Doc—in his best master of ceremonies voice—said, "We are gathered here today to honor you, Princess, for your strength, courage, and determination in your search for truth."

Strength, courage, and determination. . . . The princess smiled. Yes, Doc was right. She had never felt stronger, more courageous, or more determined in her life.

"You have made your way across stormy seas and deep sand, up steep mountains, and through dense fog," Doc continued. "You have slipped and slid, tumbled and fallen, only to rise up again and continue on. All this and more have you endured in search of truth—truth that promised to heal you and bring the peace and love you so desperately desire."

He ceremoniously adjusted his stethoscope and went on. "You have rightfully earned the honor of being here today at the Temple of Truth and of holding the treasured Sacred Scroll in your hands."

"I don't see the scroll anywhere," the princess whispered anxiously to the wizard.

"Not to worry. Everything happens in its own time," the wizard whispered back.

Chapter Eighteen

The Sacred Scroll

A HUSH came over the temple. The princess's heart was pounding so loudly she thought everyone could hear it piercing the quiet.

The wizard turned and faced the stone wall. She raised her hands high into the air. A puff of white smoke appeared.

A moment later a great rumble swelled in the wall. It seemed to vibrate the entire rotunda. The princess leaned forward and clenched the arms of the throne. Suddenly a section of wall slid open, exposing a delicate-looking, old parchment scroll affixed with a golden seal, sitting on a jewel-studded altar.

The wizard lifted the scroll from the altar like a piece of fine china and offered it to the princess, who took it and carefully removed the seal. "I've waited a long time for this moment," she said, her voice shaking ever so slightly.

"You did more than *wait*," the wizard reminded her. "Receiving the Sacred Scroll is an honor you have *earned*."

Her stomach fluttering wildly, the princess unrolled the scroll. It looked as if it had been lettered by a royal palace calligrapher, reminding the princess of the Royal Code of Feelings and Behavior for Princesses. "Shall I read it aloud?" she asked.

"Yes, dear. That would be nice," answered the wizard, who was busily putting on a pair of slightly bent, wire reading glasses she had struggled to retrieve from her pocketbook so she could look on.

The princess took a slow, deep breath to calm herself, then read aloud, "'The First Sacred Scroll.'

"The first?" she repeated, looking up from the parchment. "Isn't there only one? I didn't see any others."

"No need to discuss that now," the wizard said.

"I hope that doesn't mean what I think it means," the princess replied, looking from Doc to the wizard and back to Doc. Then she began again:

THE FIRST SACRED SCROLL

These Truths We Hold to Be Self-Evident . . .
Yet Most Often They Are Not

I

We are, first and foremost, children of the universe—whole, beautiful, perfect in every detail—for we are as the Infinite meant us to be. As such, it is our birthright to be worthy of respect and love—and our obligation to accept nothing less.

"And I never will again," said the princess, looking back up at Doc and the wizard, who both nodded in agreement. "This should have been in the Royal Code of Feelings and Behavior for Princesses that was hanging on my bedroom wall all the years I was growing up."

She lowered her eyes and continued reading:

II

As the whole of the ocean is in every droplet of water, so do we contain the whole of life. As the sea ebbs and flows, so shall we ebb and flow with the tide of life, accepting that the only constant is change, and being resolute that all is as it is meant to be, even when we know not why.

"Reading about the sea reminds me of Dolly," the princess said. "She taught me all about the sea—how to relax and let go and go with the flow, instead of struggling against it. I wish she could have been here. She would have loved this!"

III

Within the arms of weakness is strength, eager to burst free. Within the grasp of pain is pleasure, waiting just to be. And within the path of obstacles lies opportunity. For all that these teachers bring to life, shall we be ever grateful.

A look of sudden realization crossed the princess's face. "I never thought of the pain the prince caused me as being a teacher, but I guess I've learned all I've learned because of it."

"Remember, some of one's biggest lessons come from one's greatest pain," Doc replied.

The princess sighed, then looked back down and read:

IV

There is a grand design of which we are a part that does not rely upon us to be in charge of it. Everyone and everything has a rightful place in this grand design, and a reason for being.

As the princess read on, her hands and feet began to tingle, and a feeling of warmth arose in her chest. She had never felt anything quite like it.

The wizard reached down and rested her hand on the princess's shoulder. "All is well, dear. What you're feeling is a result of what you're thinking and believing."

It seemed odd to the princess that the wizard could tell what she was feeling without her having said a word. Trying to dismiss it from her mind, she turned her attention back to the scroll:

V

Experience is not always truth, for it is colored by the eyes through which it is seen. It is in the silence of our mind that we hear truth. The gentle voice that speaks to our heart like a whisper is the Creator stirring within, trying to make us aware of all that we truly are, all that we are meant to do, and all that we already know.

The princess recalled the gentle voice of the Infinite as it spoke to her heart and thought about the feeling she had in its presence. Gradually the tingling in her hands and arms crept up to the top of her head and down to the tip of her toes, and the warmth in her chest began to spread. She cupped her hand over her mouth and whispered to the wizard.

"Excuse me, but now I'm *really* feeling strange. I don't understand why. The scroll is beautiful, but it sounds so simple and obvious— I mean, it's not like I don't already know some of this."

"Knowing the truth is not enough," the wizard whispered back. "It must be felt as part of you for it to work its magic."

"Is that what's happening? The truth is becoming part of me?"

"The truth has always been part of you, but you were

not aware of it."

"As I become more aware of it, will I be able to make puffs of white smoke, like you do?" the princess asked with girlish glee.

"There will be no white smoke, dear, but there will be magic nonetheless. You'll see what I mean very soon. For now, let us continue."

VI

Each new moment is a banquet of fresh possibilities. Each day a perfect plum waiting to be picked. Again and again, shall we reap the harvest, partaking of the plenty while wasting not—for precious is all that is. And all that is, shall all too soon be all that was.

"Though all that was and all that is, is one," interjected the wizard.

The princess stopped reading and looked up at her, perplexed.

"Sorry," the wizard said apologetically. "I didn't mean to interrupt. Anyway, that's another subject for another time. Please go on, dear."

VII

When we walk upon the Path of Truth, we feel flowing through us the beauty and perfection of all that we are, of all that others are, and of all that is. Our chosen way is one of gentleness, kindness, compassion, acceptance, and appreciation. With these shall our mind be full. Such fullness of mind shall create love in our heart. And love in our heart shall create love in our life.

VIII

*When we walk upon the Path of Truth so shall we
be ever mindful that what lies within us is of far
more importance than what lies behind us or before
us. For that which lies within us is the greatest of
all treasures—the magnificence of the universe,
itself.*

Silence reigned throughout the rotunda. Not a chirp or
a word could be heard. A powerful energy pulsated
throughout the princess's body. And the feeling of warmth
continued to spread out farther and farther until it seemed
to encompass the entire rotunda and everyone in it—and to
the gardens beyond and the sky above. She felt light and
heady, yet experienced a depth of clarity that she had never
known before.

The princess suddenly became aware of why the
Sacred Scroll had affected her so profoundly. She looked
down at the parchment she held in her hands. She glanced
at Doc, the wizard, and the gallery of birds, who were
waiting eagerly.

"This is my *New Royal Code*," she announced.

All at once a puff of white smoke billowed up around
her. When it cleared, the scroll had vanished. In its place
was a lovely crystal hand mirror etched with tiny roses. The
princess was startled. "What happened to the scroll?" she
asked, alarmed. "I wanted to keep it always."

"Not to worry. I have it right here," replied the wizard,
holding up the scroll. "Now, look into the mirror, dear," she
urged.

"But all I'll see is myself. I don't understand."

"Go on, Princess. Look," Doc said, excited by a faint
ring of light becoming more and more visible like a halo
around her.

The princess complied and looked into the mirror. Beaming back at her from her own big amber eyes was a sparkle far more brilliant than any she had seen in all her life—more brilliant even than the sparkle that had once been in her adoring prince's eyes.

Suddenly Vicky's voice rang out, breaking the silence. "Are they sparkling just for us, Victoria?"

"Yes," she answered, looking deeper into the mirror and knowing it was true.

"No one can take it away from us this time. Not ever!" said the excited little voice Victoria had come to adore.

Joyful, the princess wrapped her arms tightly around herself and hugged with all her might.

Doc winked at the wizard, and the wizard smiled in satisfaction. The birds were all atwitter.

Over the commotion, Vicky said, "I have to ask you something really, really important, Victoria."

The birds settled down, and all eyes were once again on the princess.

"What is it, Vicky?" Victoria asked, dabbing happy tears from her cheek with a handkerchief the wizard had handed her.

"Do you promise to love me and cherish me in good times and bad, in sickness and in health, and all that other stuff?"

"I do," Victoria replied. "And I vow to take care of you. And to listen to you. And to try to understand."

"Will you keep anything from ever hurting me again?"

"I can't promise *that*. But I *can* promise to be there for you always and to be your best friend."

"Cross your heart and hope to die?"

"Yes, Vicky," said Victoria, setting the mirror down beside her and crossing her heart with her hand. "Cross my heart and hope to die, kiss a lizard in one try."

Victoria looked up timidly, realizing how silly she and

Vicky must sound. The wizard smiled down at her reassuringly.

Victoria took a deep breath and cleared her throat. "And do *you* promise, Vicky, to always be my bundle of wonder and innocence, my link to a happy heart?"

"I do. No matter what!"

"And do you promise to gift me with your laughter, your tears, and the sweetness of your songs?"

"I do, I do!"

Victoria pulled a single rose from one of the crystal vases and held it out adoringly in front of her. "This is for you, Vicky. A symbol of our love."

"It's for you, too, Victoria. It's *for* us and *from* us! And not 'cause somebody else stopped giving them to us, either!"

The princess sprang to her feet. "I never imagined I could be this happy without a prince! You were right," she said to the wizard. "When you feel the truth as part of you, it *is* like magic!"

She waved the flower in the air and gracefully turned this way and that, swooping down low and reaching up high in a spirited dance that came from somewhere deep inside her. All the while she had no idea that a halo of radiant light was now glowing all around her.

The birds chirped and tweeted at the top of their little voices, flapping their wings and hopping around. Doc flapped and hopped and "whoo-whoo'd" with the best of them. The wizard, laughing heartily, joined in the fun.

In the midst of the festivities, the princess suddenly remembered her fairy tale and was puzzled. She called to Doc. "You told me when I started on this journey that when I got to the Temple of Truth, I'd be well on my way to having my fairy tale come true."

"And so you are, Princess," he replied. "For to truly love another, one must first love oneself."

"But aren't fairy tales supposed to have a prince in them?"

"Yes, when they're the kind read to children at bedtime. Real-life fairy tales are supposed to have happily ever afters—with or without a prince."

The princess thought about why for so much of her life she had longed for a prince—in fact, had often felt like nothing without one. She had needed a prince to love her, needed the sparkle in his eyes to be happy and to feel beautiful, special, and loveable. It just goes to show how wrong one can be, she thought, recalling what she had learned about princes and rescues and love. She now knew that as much as she still wanted a prince *in* her life, he could never again *be* her life and that she loved herself enough to make herself happy—prince or no prince.

"You once told me that my fairy tale can come true, but it might be a different one than I first envisioned," she said. "I'm beginning to understand what you meant."

She sat down on the edge of the throne, tilted her head, and clasped her hands to her cheek. "But I still want a prince who will make my heart go pitter-patter and my knees grow weak when he gazes into my eyes."

"A romantic notion, to be sure, but there's a lot more to choosing a real Prince Charming than gazing into the eyes of a stranger and feeling that he is the one."

"Then how will I know him?"

"By the pureness of his spirit and the fullness of his heart."

"You mean he will be like the Sacred Scroll says—gentle, kind, compassionate, and everything?"

"Yes," Doc replied. "Toward himself as well as others. For one loves another as one loves oneself—with gentleness and acceptance, or with harshness and rejection."

"Is that the secret of true love?" asked the princess.

"Part of it," Doc answered. Another part is liking."

"Liking?"

"Yes, for one cannot love a person one does not like. And that means liking who the other person *really is*, not who *you want or need* him or her to be."

The princess thought for a moment, then asked eagerly, "Are there any more parts to the secret?"

"Yes, many more, such as trusting and sharing and being best friends. True love means freedom and growth rather than ownership and limitations. It means peace rather than turmoil, and safety instead of fear," Doc said, beginning to talk faster. "It means understanding, loyalty, encouragement, commitment, connectedness, and—ah, this is an especially important part for *you,* Princess—respect. For when one is not treated with respect, there is inevitably pain—a deep, unsettling, destructive, nerve-frazzling kind that is never a part of the beauty that is true love."

"I know about *that* only too well. And now I know that it was my obligation to accept nothing less than respect, like the scroll says. But even true love surely must have its difficult moments. I mean, sometimes people get upset and say things—"

"Yes, but one can be upset about something another person says or does without disliking and mistreating the person who said or did it. True love means agreeing to disagree as friends and teammates, rather than as adversaries or competitors—for true love is not about warring or winning." His voice grew louder and deeper, and he stood tall, his chest puffing out like a peacock. "And it is never demeaning, never cruel, never attacking, never violent. It makes a home a castle, never a prison. True love—"

"Doc . . . Doc," the wizard called insistently.

The owl abruptly stopped talking and flapped his wing over his mouth. "Oops, I guess I got a little carried away," he said, lowering his wing. "Sorry, that tends to happen when I'm talking about my favorite subject."

"That's all right. It's *my* favorite subject, too," the princess replied. Then she sighed deeply. "It's funny. I've been dreaming of finding true love all my life, but I didn't even know what it was."

"Which is the reason why you had difficulty finding it. One cannot find what one is looking for unless one first knows what it is."

She sat silently, her eyes filling with tears. Finally she said, "My fairy tale kept me believing that what I had was true love." She shifted uncomfortably in her seat. "I believed in the ecstacy of the fairy tale in spite of the agony of the reality. I stayed and stayed, waiting and hoping my fairy tale would still come true."

"That was then, and this is now. Your fairy tale can still come true if it is the right one."

The princess remembered what the Sacred Scroll said about fullness of mind and how love in one's heart creates love in one's life, and she imagined what the future might hold for her.

"True love sounds even better than I ever dreamed—except for the part about no heart going pitter-patter and no weak knees. That's so sad. It's more than sad—it's downright depressing!"

Doc smiled. "I didn't say your heart wouldn't flutter and your knees wouldn't turn to jelly. Only that choosing a prince to love requires you to consider more than your fluctuating anatomy—which by the way can keep you from noticing important signposts."

The princess blushed and tried to stifle a giggle. Then she grew quiet. Doc, the wizard, and the birds waited patiently.

Finally, her voice quivering with emotion, the princess said, "I have a *new* fairy tale. A *different* fairy tale. A *better* fairy tale. It's that I live happily ever after and I find true love with a prince who's living happily ever after, and we celebrate our happiness together!"

"You've come a long way, Princess," Doc said. "You once *needed* to love *in order* to feel good. Now you can *choose* to love *because* you feel good."

"Will we live in perfect harmony, my prince and I?" she asked dreamily, clasping her hands to her cheek.

"It will be perfect in its imperfection."

She could have guessed the answer to that one, she thought. "And will our hearts beat as one?"

"No, but your hearts will beat together, as two who feel as one."

"Oh, that sounds so wonderful," the princess said. "But I don't know how I will ever find him in that great big world out there."

"Not to worry," the wizard said. "There are still many things you do not know, dear—but you will."

"Oh, *no*," the princess said, slumping back farther into the throne. "I had a feeling when I saw that the Sacred Scroll said 'The First . . . '"

"You were quite right," Doc replied. "One's journey never ends."

"I thought I was finished with difficult climbs and potholes and pebbles that roll beneath my feet and running smack dab into big boulders. Isn't that what this commencement is all about?"

"On the contrary, commencement means beginning."

"I really don't want to ask this—but what is it the beginning of?" she asked anxiously.

"Putting one's newly attained knowledge to practical use. An important part of learning truth is living it."

The princess stared down at the soft velvet beneath her and stroked it with her fingers.

"What's the matter?" Doc asked.

"I guess it's just that I've come so far, and now I feel

I have so far yet to go."

"You do? To get to where?"

"I'm not sure. Someplace that'll feel like I've gotten to where I was supposed to go, I guess."

"Most of life is the *going*—not the *getting there,* for when one gets to where one thought one was going, one inevitably feels the need to go somewhere else. It's all an adventure, Princess, an enlightening adventure. Be happy. The best is yet to come."

Suddenly the princess became aware of what sounded like muffled music of some sort. She listened closely, trying to figure out where it was coming from, then looked suspiciously at her paisley bag lying on the floor next to the throne.

"Go ahead, dear," the wizard said.

When she pulled the bag open, the crisp, tinkling notes of one lone flute sprang into the air. Perplexed as to what had happened to "Someday My Prince Will Come," she reached in and pulled out her little music box. But it turned out not to be *her* little music box at all! This one had a single figure on top that looked like her. It was swaying to the music, gracefully turning this way and that, swooping down low and reaching up high in a spirited dance that seemed to come from somewhere deep inside it.

All at once there were two flutes. Then a piccolo. The little figure swayed farther and reached higher and swooped lower, as if her dance had been infused with the potpourri of lively sounds spiraling around her. Clarinets joined in, and the music grew stronger and fuller. The figure seemed to come to life as it waltzed gaily and twirled with abandon around and around the top of the music box.

"What's going on here?" the princess asked, assuming that the wizard was up to her usual tricks.

The wizard's face was beaming. "Keep watching, dear."

The music grew fuller yet, and sweeter, as violins began to play. The figure's impassioned dance mesmerized the princess. The music continued to grow stronger and stronger and fuller and fuller. It swelled within her, more and more, until finally, she and the music became one. Wide-eyed, she looked at the wizard.

"It's not over yet. It gets even better," the wizard said, raising her voice above the symphony of sounds.

The princess was dismayed. "Better! How could it possibly get any better than this?"

"You'll see. Look again."

When she did, to her astonishment, the little princess figure was dancing in the arms of a handsome prince. Eloquently they twirled and dipped and glided in perfect unison. Cellos joined in, and the music continued to build. The little couple whirled around the top of the music box, faster and faster. As more instruments joined in, the music got even fuller, richer, and stronger until the entire rotunda reverberated with the sound of timpani drums, and the beveled-glass wall panels vibrated with the crashing of cymbals. The little royal couple, laughing uncontrollably, toppled into each other's arms.

Stunned, the princess looked back at the wizard, who was standing tall, clearly proud of her handiwork. "It's a little commencement gift," she said. "A reminder of your new fairy tale."

The princess jumped up and clasped the little music box to her chest. "I love it! I'll play it over and over. Each time it will remind me that I am whole and that the love in my heart shall create love in my life, and that everything will be *as* it is meant to be, *when* it is meant to be—for everything happens as it is meant to happen and in its own time," she stated as if she had known it her whole life.

The wizard was highly gratified by the princess's reply. "You have learned your lessons well, dear."

"Thank you," the princess replied, beaming with pride. "Now I have only to live them."

"Yes!" the wizard said.

"Yes!" Doc said.

"And I will—perfectly."

"Perfectly?" the wizard asked doubtfully.

"Perfectly?" Doc asked with obvious concern.

But the princess said nothing. The only sound was a sudden flurry of hushed cheeping and peeping. She lifted her eyebrows, trying with all her might to hold back a smile that begged to spring free.

"Yes, *perfectly*—as perfectly as any perfectly imperfect princess can live them!" she said finally, exploding into laughter.

Doc and the wizard burst out laughing, too. The birds outdid themselves with their chirping and tweeting, flapping and hopping around. They all encircled the princess in a ring of joy.

After awhile the wizard said, "The time has come for you to go."

"Now? But I'm having so much fun."

"Yes, dear—now," the wizard replied.

"But *where* will I go?" the princess asked, remembering having asked the same question when she first left the prince and set out on the path—and realizing that although her heart was pounding as it had that day long ago, this time she was more excited than afraid.

"You will continue on the Path of Truth," Doc answered. "Down the other side of the mountain and on to the adventure that awaits you."

"The *enlightening* adventure. Right, Doc?"

"Yes, Princess, for there are always new trails to blaze and new songs to sing. Ah, that reminds me— We have a special outdoor musical send-off planned."

"That sounds wonderful," the princess replied, picking

up her paisley bag and placing the little music box inside. Then she scooped up the birdiegrams from the top of the pedestal where Doc had placed them and slipped them carefully into the bag along with the Sacred Scroll, which the wizard had rolled up and handed to her.

"May I take this, too?" she asked, reaching for the mirror.

"Of course," the wizard replied. "I conjured it up especially for you, dear—with the roses and all."

The princess tucked the mirror into the wool scarf that held her little glass slippers and closed her bag.

Arm-in-arm, she and the wizard made their way across the rotunda, with Doc hovering close at their side and the birds crisscrossing happily behind them. Through the foyer, past the courtyard, and out the white wrought-iron gates into the late afternoon sun they went.

"Thank you all so much for everything!" the princess said, setting down her bag and hugging Doc and the wizard, not wanting to let go. "Will I ever see you again?" she asked hopefully. But before anyone could answer, she remembered. "I know," she said, recalling Dolly's parting words: 'Those you carry in your heart are forever near.'"

Ecstatic, Doc retrieved his banjo and straw hat from his black bag and patted the hat onto his head. He began strumming and singing:

> As you travel near and far,
> No matter where you are,
> Remember what your heart always knew:
> That fairy tales really *can* come true.

A chorus of jubilant voices joined in. The princess listened for a moment, then quickly hugged Doc and the wizard again. She picked up her paisley bag and looked tenderly at the loving group before her. She wanted to memorize the moment—exactly how everyone looked and how she felt.

"Keep the music playing," she said in a voice as melodious as the sweetest song ever sung.

"Keeping the music playing will be entirely up to you now, Princess," Doc replied, fanning out his wings high in the air so they towered above her. "Go forth and live your highest truth, Princess."

"I will," she replied with conviction, the beautiful ring of light around her glowing brighter than ever.

She turned and walked from the mountaintop, her excitement about the wonderful, new life she was about to begin growing with each step. Yet a touch of sadness kept tugging at her. Not sure if or when she would ever again see her beloved friends, she stopped and turned to wave one final good-bye.

To her amazement, everything and everyone was gone! The temple, Doc, the wizard, and the birds—all gone! How could it be? She rubbed her eyes in disbelief and looked again. There was nothing at all.

She took a deep, calming breath, then another. Gradually she became aware of a distant, familiar whisper, echoing softly from mountaintop to mountaintop. She listened intently.

"Believe . . . believe . . . believe . . ." it said.

At that very moment—ever so faintly—a new rendition of Doc's song "Fairy Tales Really *Can* Come True" began to play. At first the princess was perplexed. A moment passed. Then like a lightning bolt, it hit her. The music was coming from within herself!

With a smile on her lips, a spring in her step, and a song in her heart, she descended into a glorious sunset of a thousand colors.

The Beginning

A Personal Word From the Author . . .

Dear Friend,

As a woman who spent years in pain and emerged happy, stronger, and wiser, I encourage you to follow the Path of Truth. It will lead you to a peaceful, joyous place where every day will feel like a gift and your laughter will be far more plentiful than your tears.

I am thankful that my own journey out of darkness has led me to that peaceful, joyous place, and I derive great satisfaction from casting light along the way for those who wish to follow—by lecturing and writing, and as senior editor at Wilshire Book Company, by seeking out and helping to make available unique books that teach, inspire, and empower. My favorites are allegorical tales that explore the meaning of life and love, and offer insights to understanding, accepting, and loving oneself and the universe, such as *The Princess Who Believed in Fairy Tales* and a very special, powerful book entitled *The Knight in Rusty Armor* by Robert Fisher.

I am excited about having this opportunity to introduce you to the knight. He will help you along your journey and will have great appeal to the men in your life, who will identify with him and learn invaluable lessons from his story.

The original manuscript for this delightful, insightful fantasy stood out among the thousands we receive each year. I took a personal interest in it, and it has become one of Wilshire's bestselling titles. Anyone who has ever struggled with the meaning of life and love will discover profound wisdom and truth as the knight's story unfolds.

I invite you to join him as he faces a life-changing dilemma upon discovering that his shining armor cannot be removed. As he searches for a way to free himself, he receives guidance from the wise sage Merlin the Magician, who encourages the knight to embark on the most difficult crusade of his life.

With the help of an intuitive little creature named

Squirrel and a loyal, clever pigeon, Rebecca, the knight travels the Path of Truth where he meets his real self for the first time. As he passes through the castles of Silence, Knowledge, and Will and Daring, he confronts the universal truths that govern his life—and ours.

The knight's journey reflects our own—filled with hope and despair, belief and disillusionment, happiness and sadness. His insights become our insights as we follow along on this intriguing adventure of self-discovery.

The Knight is more than a book. It's an experience that will expand your mind, touch your heart, and nourish your soul. It is available at all bookstores or directly from Wilshire Book Company, 12015 Sherman Road, No. Hollywood, CA 91605-3781 for $5.00 plus $2.00 S/H (CA residents $7.41).

If you would like to accompany the princess as she continues on her journey of self-discovery in a forthcoming sequel to *The Princess Who Believed in Fairy Tales,* please send your name and address to *The Princess* at the address above.

Until we meet again, my fellow traveler, follow Doc's wise advice: *Go forth and live your highest truth.* And be ready to hope a new hope, dream a new dream, and believe . . . believe . . . believe again in yourself, in life, and in love.